THE GOLDEN MONEY TREE

THE GOLDEN MONEY TREE

MONEY TREE

MALCOLM KENDRICK

Matador
9 Priory Business Park,
Wistow Road, Kibworth Beauchamp,
Leicestershire, LE8 0RX
Tel: 0116 279 2299
Email: books@troubador.co.uk
Web: www.troubador.co.uk/matador
Twitter: @matadorbooks

ISBN 978 1838591 359

British Library Cataloguing in Publication Data.
A catalogue record for this book is available from the British Library.

Printed and bound by CPI Group (UK) Ltd, Croydon, CR0 4YY
Typeset in 11pt Caslon Pro by Troubador Publishing Ltd, Leicester, UK

Matador is an imprint of Troubador Publishing Ltd

·

The Golden Money Tree has been harder to write than I anticipated, two years from its inception to arriving in bookshops; would I do it again, no; has it been worth it, yes.

All my family, when I am no more, will have something to look back upon and remember me by my book. It is to them and my heirs I dedicate this book.

CONTENTS

If you can keep your head when all about you
Are losing theirs and blaming it on you
If you can trust yourself when all men doubt you
But make allowances for their doubting too,
If you can wait and not be tired of waiting,
Or being lied about, don't deal in lies,
Or being hated, don't give way to hating,
And yet don't look too good, nor talk too wise
If you can dream – and not make dreams your master,
If you can think and not make thoughts your aim;
If you can meet with Triumph and Disaster
And treat those two imposters just the same;
If you can bear to hear the truth you've spoken
Twisted by knaves to make a trap for fools
Or watch the things you gave your life to broken
And stop to build 'em up with worn out tools
Yours is the Earth and everything that's in it,
And – which is more – you'll be a Man, my son!

Form 'If…' by Rudyard Kipling

CHAPTER ONE

MY FORMATIVE YEARS

I remember starting school: Gelligraig School, Abertillery. I was three. A little time after this I was allowed to walk home. My mother would meet me half way. On one particular day as I headed back to our house, I saw my dad walking towards me instead, wearing his RAF uniform: it was wartime. I felt so proud of him; I ran towards him; we both had broad smiles on our faces. I ran into his arms; he picked me up, holding me close to his body, giving me a big *cwtch* (that's Welsh for hug).

My earliest memories are almost all like that – happy. My mother would regularly say to me that her mother would dote over me, as I was her only grandchild at the time. My father's parents would also be the same. We all lived in Abertillery, only a few streets away from each other.

Both my grandfathers were underground miners working in the valley pits. Both had large families to feed; in the 1920s and the days of the great depression, that was difficult. Grandfather Daniels (on my mother's side) was an underground manager at Six Bells Colliery, when an explosion took place and many lives were lost.

My parents were both born in the town. They had to get married, as she was in the early stages of pregnancy with me. I think to keep it quiet, but also to look for work, they moved to Luton to join his younger brother Billy, who at the time was working as a bus driver. Uncle Bill got dad in as a conductor, and he rented a flat at 21 Whitefield Avenue, Sundon, where I was born on 3rd October 1939.

However, war had broken out by then. My parents' plans went up in smoke. My father went off to war and my mother took me back home to Abertillery. She stayed with her mother until my father came home on leave, when they rented a little old terraced cottage: 3 Parsons Row.

My father was training as a rear gunner. During that time, he had an air crash in the north of England; his leg was broken and he finished up in hospital for months. I can remember him coming to see us at Parsons Row. He arrived at the end of the row of cottages in a posh car driven by an RAF chauffeur and accompanied by an RAF nurse. All the neighbours were out crowding around the car. The nurse stepped out and went to the back door to open it to help my dad out. He stepped out on crutches in his uniform. I can remember it as if it was today. I looked at him with a big smile. I was so proud he was my dad.

He only stayed a couple of hours, as they had to take him back to hospital for him to fully recover. At the time, once you had an air crash you did not have to fly again. However, on his recovery, he returned to his training as a bomber gunner. On passing out, you were given the rank of sergeant and posted to a squadron: he was posted to 158 Squadron at RAF Lissett.

On reporting to the squadron office, he was interviewed by his commanding officer. My father said he did not want to fly again (by this time he had learnt that the chances of a gunner surviving were very slim). However the squadron was short of gunners, as it was continually losing them. The CO persuaded my father to fly. Pointing to a large blackboard on the wall, where all the pilots and there crew were listed, he said, 'You can pick any one of the pilots you want to fly with.' My father looked up at the board and didn't know any of the names from Adam. But he noted that one pilot had a DFC (Distinguished Flying Cross) next to his name. He pointed to Fight Lieutenant Bridger DFC and said, 'He will do me.'

Bridger turned out to be a very experienced and courageous pilot. He had just come off flying Lysander aircraft for the SOE (Special Operations Executive), taking important people and secret agents into France at night. He would land on fields that were marked out with burning flame markers, coming in over the tops of trees (the Lysanders would often come back with tree branches caught up in their undercarriage).

The day after this discussion, my father and the rest of F/Lt Bridger's crew were sent on a midnight raid in a brand new Halifax that had only been delivered the day before. They unloaded their bombs on the heart of Germany, but on their return, searchlights picked them out and the aircraft was hit by flack. One engine caught fire and had to be closed down. Slowly losing height, they had to make it back over the North Sea. Their route took them across Mont-Rigi in the Ardennes, a notorious grave of Bomber crews returning from missions. As they approached the mountains, F/Lt Bridger realised they were not going to make it. He told the crew he was going to bring the plane down. At the time, the area was remote forest. He instructed the crew to take the brace position, and they all waited in fear as F/Lt Bridger DFC did his best to avoid disaster.

He did so, bringing the aircraft down in the middle of a forest but keeping it upright. My father was trapped at the back. Both his legs had multiple fractures and he had one eye hanging out.

The wireless operator, Sergeant Scudamore, who was also a trained rear gunner, worked his way down to where my father was trapped. Despite his own injuries – he had severe gashes to the head and was losing a lot of blood – he managed to drag him back and out of the Halifax. My father owed his life to Scudamore, and never forgot it. (The sergeant was also a successful National Hunt jockey. My father enjoyed a punt on the horses, and I remember many times when he was studying the racing form in the papers and came across the name Michael Scudamore, he would look up and say to me how he saved his life.) He also owed his life to F/Lt Bridger, for his skill, calm and courage in landing the plane.

As some of the crew were badly injured they decided to all stick together and wait to be found by the Germans the following morning.

My father was taken to a German hospital and treated well. The surgeons worked wonders on his leg fractures. He was then sent to a Stalag Luft prison camp (one operated by the Luftwaffe for captured aircrew), where if you were British they abided by the Geneva Convention. Two years after his capture, he was repatriated on the ship Arundel Castle with other prisoners who were deemed of no use to the war effort, exchanged with German POWs.

In the meantime, back home, my mother was coping with bringing up me and my two younger sisters.

On my father's return home to Abertillery as an RAF Warrant Officer, all the streets had flags and bunting hung out from bedroom windows. As before, he arrived in an RAF car accompanied by a nurse, in his uniform and using a walking stick. He came to our little cottage terrace house with all our family there to greet him, and sat down in an armchair with me on his lap – I felt even prouder than ever – while he told us about life in a prisoner of war camp. Then he went upstairs with my mother.

They weren't there long. Both soon came downstairs again with blank faces. I could sense the change in atmosphere, but because of my innocence I could not understand why. It transpired that my mother had said to him that she now loved another man.

Being a small community, it did not take long for the gossip to get around. The following morning our neighbours had taken down the flags and bunting. In the 1940s it was thought of as a crime, after having sworn your Christian marriage vows to each other at the altar, to break them.

My dad still wanted to patch it up. I remember rows when we were all sitting at the dinner table. I remember one day the 'other man', Jack Hughes, came to the bottom of the garden enquiring about my mother. My dad went down the garden path and gave him a good thumping. I shan't say in this book what I still think of Hughes – the words are unprintable.

The inevitable happened: divorce. It went on for ages. My mother was cited as the guilty party. My father said that he was told that if he wished he could take all three of us, but it was best if the two girls stayed with my mother and he kept me. Who else would want three children from someone else's marriage on a permanent basis? It was agreed that I would spend my school holidays with my mother and my sisters. The three of us were then divided up as if we were cattle and not thought of as children. This separation was the beginning of the saddest part of my life.

CHAPTER TWO
MY DARKEST TIMES

My dad went back to live in Luton, where he started his own business as a taxi operator. When he came to collect me (by train) from Abertillery, however, we did not go to Luton but St Albans, where I was to live with his cousin. Aunt Gladys and my Uncle Norman had a three-bedroom semi at Park Street, a small village on the busy A5 just south of St Albans. She had four nice, pretty girls aged from around 20 to 16 (the youngest, my cousin June). I shared a bedroom with two of them. Aunt Gladys gave me my own bed. She was really fantastic to me, and I felt her comfort very much – but I never said so. Having just being separated from my mother, I was quiet and withdrawn, tending to accept everything as I had no choice, although there was plenty of confusion buzzing around in my head.

This move took place at the start of the school summer holidays, which in those days lasted around eight weeks, leaving me what they thought would be time to adjust and settle down. But I felt very alone, remote and isolated.

There were also better times. There were fields of open countryside behind my Aunt's house, and a small copse in one. I would clamber over the fence at the back of the house and make for the copse. Here I could feel relaxed and content in my isolation. I would also collect eggs from the chicken coop in my Aunt's garden, and she would come with me and talk to me. Her comforting words would put me in a better frame of mind. She would take me on a Saturday morning to Saint Albans market, and buy me a small toy or perhaps buy some small baby chicks to take back for her chicken run. On a Wednesday my dad would come over to see me.

At the end of the school holidays I started at Park Street Infants' School. I could walk to it over footpaths and fields, and enjoyed this (except the last part of the way home, which was uphill and which I found tiring). I felt comfortable in school, especially at play time when I would play marbles with the other boys.

As regards academic achievement – well, the best I can say is that I was bottom of the class. If you were dyslexic in the 1940s you were considered a dunce and an irritation for asking too many questions. On his Wednesday afternoon visits, my dad would meet me at school and walk back with me through the fields. I still couldn't spell my own name: I remember him trying to drum it into me by repeating the spelling over and over again and asking me to repeat it. M,a,l,c... I got there eventually.

It was about this time my Aunt Gladys noticed me being very tired when I came home from school. I was no Billy Bunter but I was overweight. She said to my father that there was something wrong, and we went to see the local doctor. He sent me to Dr Franklyn, a heart specialist at St Bartholomew's Hospital in London. They kept me in for a week.

Around this time, my father took me back to Luton to live with him in a flat at 24 Rothesay Road. He led me in, and I was faced by a woman that he had married. I think he introduced her to me as 'Aunty'. I remember her standing by the fireplace with her breast out, feeding a baby, who turned out to be Stephen, her second child.

My mind was crazily mixed up – but there was nothing I could do about it. So I had to meekly accept it – with one exception: I never ever in my whole life called her Aunty, mum, or mother. There were times when to avoid causing embarrassment, I would avoid calling her anything. Now, I understand that it was not her fault. My parents' divorce came before she met my father. But, growing up, I found that hard to grasp.

CHAPTER THREE

SCHOOL LIFE IN LUTON

I started at the local junior school in Dunstable Rd. I became a member of the school cubs, but most of all would enjoy football lessons on a Friday afternoon. My dad would come and watch me play. It was just one marauding pack of boys all trying to get a kick at the ball – one time, he called me over and said, 'Don't try to kick it in the pack; stand outside and wait for it to come out.' It was good advice.

My father and his new family were on a council waiting list for the allocation of a house. My joining him gave them extra points which moved them up the list, so it wasn't long before they received a letter allocating them a new-build three-bedroom house. I shall talk about this place and my life there in the next chapter: in this one, we are staying at school.

I moved to Stopsley Junior Mixed School. On the first day, I was interviewed by the headmaster, Mr Benson. He was the first teacher I found inspiring. He had a favourite saying, 'You young monkey', if you were messing about. Occasionally, when he had a teacher off, he would come into the class and teach us. I remember one English class, where he made it so simple, easy and interesting. One example: he drew on the class large blackboard, in large capital letters, the word MOTOR, then said that in order to help you remember how to spell it, think of a car with the Os as two big headlights.

This worked wonders for me: a five-letter word which I could remember in an instant, when I was still having trouble with three-letter ones!

I was put in class B, the middle one. As I walked in, the class gave me a good reception: I remember the boys sitting at the front desks asking me if I played football. When I said yes, they said 'Bring your togs in tomorrow as we have a match against Class A.'

My togs were cleaned up with fresh dubbin ready for the game, and I waited at school all morning in anticipation. The afternoon came around and I was put into the team at my favourite position, centre forward. I remember walking out together with our rivals, through the back of the school grounds to Stopsley Park. I looked around to see if my dad was there, as he had said he was coming to watch and had even promised me two bob for every goal I scored. He was.

The match kicked off. Our rivals immediately put us under pressure with their continuous attacking. As centre forward, I would hang around the half way line waiting for one of my team to blast the ball up field to me. The A team had two defending backs, big, tall boys who both went on to play for the school. They would stand with their legs wide apart, and when I tried to get around them, they would rob me of the ball. After a while my father called me over and said, 'Next time you face one of them, kick it through his legs and run around him.'

I can see clearly in my mind even now… I waited till someone booted the ball up field to me. I got the ball under control, then turned to face the left full-back, a boy named Barton (who was also bright: he went on to the grammar school). I kicked the ball through his legs and sprinted round him. Quick as a flash, he turned and was after me. I ran as fast as I could, keeping the ball under control and just managing to keep ahead of him. Now the goal-keeper was squaring up to face me. I flicked my eyes up to pick my shot and placed the ball past him to score.

The whole B team erupted. We were one up, and we had never been one up against Form A before. I was so chuffed. I went on to use dad's method successfully for the rest of the game and scored a hat trick (Dad gladly paid up, though six shillings was a lot of money then for a working man.) We won 3–1. What happened next I will never forget: my whole team picked me up and carried me over their heads off the pitch and out of the park through the school gate.

Wonderful! But it turned out to be the last football match I would ever take part in again. Dr Franklin, the heart specialist I had visited in London, sent a recommendation of no more sport for the rest of my school days.

I was eventually moved down to the C form. This was a real cultural change; the class was unruly, and the teacher, Mr Oxley, a very tall, thin, bespectacled man, had difficulty keeping order. He often had to resort to the cane.

I was (and still am) a chatterbox. I remember one day Mr Oxley decided he was going to cure me of this. I was quietly whispering to the boy sitting next to me when Mr Oxley called me out to the front of the class and said, 'Hold your hand out.' The whole class, watching in silence, knew what this meant.

I knew what I had to do. When having the cane, keep your hand flat and bend the thumb back as far as you can, to avoid the thumb taking the full force of the cane. Don't try taking your hand away or you risk the chance of getting two whacks. I held my hand straight out. Mr Oxley lifted the cane up above his head, then with a big swish brought it down as hard as he could. Wow, that stung.

That day, for some reason, I ended up getting this punishment three times.

I didn't cry – that was a matter of pride. I went home with bruised fingers, feeling right miserable, but never said a word to anyone there, either.

Despite this, I think the cane never caused me or my contemporaries any real harm. Actually, I consider we grew up as better people, for it kept law and order in the classroom. Having said that, Mr Oxley failed to cure me of chattering!

At the end of the year we sat the 'eleven plus' exam for entrance to a grammar school. The teachers tried to impress upon us how important it was to do our best, but it did not mean a lot to me. I didn't receive any special private tuition or home coaching, and I was never one to do homework…

Around 10% of us went on to Luton Grammar School. The rest of us went to Stopsley Secondary Modern. It was only about a quarter of a mile away, an attractive newly built brick building within its own green grounds and gardens where the boys could learn about practical gardening. It had its own sports field with football pitches, and in the summer a running track could be marked out. It was really two schools in one, as the girls studied in the left-hand side classrooms, and the boys in the right-hand side ones. Between them was a huge hall, which could be used for big occasions like school plays, but which also served as the boys' dinner hall, as it had its own kitchens.

Whoever planned this school and its method of education deserves full praise. Going to Stopsley Senior Secondary Modern School was the best start that someone like me could have. It prepared me well for life to come as a useful citizen for our nation. It had only been open three years, and the teachers who taught us were very enthusiastic. The headmaster, Mr Daws, was the school's first, and was very proud of this.

I started in the B form. As far as I can remember the A form had French lessons while we did woodwork. Mr Frank Walker taught me woodwork all through the school. We started with all the tools; how to look after them and the names of all the parts. Slowly he got us making things, starting with a tent peg and then a garden dibber. We learnt how to make all the right joints, just like a cabinet maker, and in our final year we were all permitted to go onto a wood-turning lathe and make a bowl. I used a piece of oak. We were allowed to buy the finished product and take the bowl home. I loved these lessons.

Our geography teacher was Mr Butler. He stood just under six feet, was plump-faced with, let's say, a wide waistline. He was mainly distinguished by his hat: a flat peaked one as worn by the common man in the 1920s. He made geography very interesting, showing lots of films on topics like exploring up the Amazon. If he thought we were interested, he would describe things in great detail. We also had him for gardening lessons, which he would take outside, giving us practical tuition. He was a jovial character – but also had a cane and would soak it in water to give it more whip. I think he preferred not to use it; for example, if he noticed you were talking in class he would call you out to the front, at the same time swishing his cane in one hand. He would hand you the cane and say, 'Go up to the washrooms and give this a good soaking.' You'd go and do that, then bring it back – and often he would then let you off, as he knew you'd learnt your lesson already.

There was the PE master, Mr Milner, a pleasant wrinkle-faced man starting to show his age. I remember watching the boys being taken by

Mr Milner in the winter cross country running from the school, out through the back gates and onto the green chalk downs that ran along overlooking the grammar school. He would run with the boys and try to ensure nobody took any short cuts. The winner nearly always was Roland Brown, winning with ease and plenty to spare – except when someone did manage to find a short cut.

Mr Milner rarely gave the cane – instead, his punishment would be physical, such as running around the school island twice or doing push-ups in the gym with the other boys looking on, laughing. Despite his advancing years, he could jump on the spring-board and somersault over the box. Excused games, I still had to attend and watch – what a waste of four years, when you think what else I could have achieved in that time (I was once considered to have some talent at painting). Mr Milner also taught us hand crafts: basket weaving, lino cutting for making prints, and much more.

The art teacher, Mr Boston, nicknamed Bomber Boston, was an ex-paratrooper who had been dropped into Arnhem. Almost bald and with a snappy walk, he had real charisma. He was prepared to joke with the boys when they were misbehaving and normally won them around to his way of thinking. More about him later.

Mr Brown, who taught English, was a rather serious personality who had difficulty instilling discipline. If the class were getting out of control, he would go red in the face and call someone out to have the cane, which he always gave you on your backside. One day, he called two boys out. Both these boys were always somewhat rebellious; the first one bent down and took his punishment, but the second stepped forward and when he was asked to bend down he refused. Mr Brown grabbed him by his arms and wrestled with him to try to get him over his knees while sitting in his armchair to administer the punishment. He did eventually succeed, but it felt like something from Tom Brown's Schooldays.

I enjoyed most of the lessons, especially the practical ones – woodwork, art, science, craft, geography and gardening – basically things that I was good at. I could be rowdy in class sometimes, but underneath I was a loner. Outside class I preferred my own space and to be left alone, often to pine to be with my mother and sisters back in Abertillery. I used to go to them in the long school holiday, and it would take around two months to get over it.

In your first year at this school, you had the chance of a second bite of the eleven plus exam. If I remember rightly, we all had to take it. Guess what? I failed again.

In your second year you could take the examination for entry for Luton Technical College, which was a kind of half-way house between my existing school and the local grammar school. I had heard about the sort of things undertaken by the students there, and this inspired me to want to attend, so I put my name down for the entrance exam. Again, I failed. I was disappointed and envious of the boys that passed, of whom I thought 'They are going places in life.' I had, however, done next to nothing for the exam. I was beginning to learn that the world didn't owe me anything and that I would have to work for everything I wanted to achieve.

By year three I was now in the upper part of the school. This made me think I was a senior boy. I even had a space allotted to me in the school bike shed! I started to improve my position in class and to take more interest in the more difficult subjects. However, on the English front I was still absolutely hopeless. If I couldn't spell a word, which happened once at least once on every line I wrote, I would ask the teacher how to spell it and he would say, 'Look it up in the dictionary.' To me, that's counterproductive: take for example the word *Knife*. To me it should have started with the letter N, so looking in the dictionary, I would never find it. As a result I wasted half the lesson.

I was much better at maths. Sometimes our form teacher Mr Tassey would sit me and another boy, I think his name was Martin, at the front of the class and write questions for us to answer. It was a race between us, and it was 50/50 as to who finished first. I also discovered chess. During the dinner break one of the classrooms was allocated for chess. Mr Walker, the woodwork teacher, would normally be present. He loved a game of chess and we all loved to play against him. There was a school chess team and I was selected to be in it – at last I could take part in something to represent the school. When there was a game on, I was allowed to leave class half way through the afternoon.

There were also other activities in the dinner break. There were school plays and, unusual for schools at that time, training for boxing. The boxing would take place in a large open area just outside the dining hall. There was a punch bag standing on a weighted base supported by a flexible rod. The school was very proud of the three gifted Bowler brothers who between them held the schools ABA titles for their age and weight. Douglas Wright, a good classmate friend of mine, who lived just down the road from me, went on to box in the schools ABA final.

Every year the school would have its own boxing tournament, organised by Bomber Boston. It would hire a full-size boxing ring on a plinth about 3-ft high. Any boy could enter if he wished to (but not me: nothing to do with my medical condition; I was scared!) Boston would match the boys of each year against each other according to his assessment for an even match, and the rest of us would be seated around the ring and allowed to encourage the boxers. Though the boys wore headgear for protection, I remember some real slugging matches with blood everywhere, usually from nose-bleeds. Most of the boys were very brave and would keep going forward. However Bomber was always on the watch and would stop a fight without question if he thought it was necessary: he was very caring of the boys.

He wouldn't stand nonsense, however. Once he was on playground duty during dinner time. We were lined up ready to march back into school, when three or four boys started messing about. Bomber went straight over, I imagine to give them a good talking to, and they started to attack him. He wasn't having any of that: single-handedly he fought back, though with a calm control. He didn't punch them but used the flat palms of his hands, slapping them around the ears and head. He soon had them under control, with all the rest of the school watching in silent amusement.

At Christmas time, Mr Dawes, the headmaster, would hire films. He knew what boys enjoyed the most: Charlie Chaplin, the Keystone Cops, Laurel and Hardy. We watched and laughed, sitting in the big hall.

Then it was my last year before having to leave to find employment – the school leaving age was 15 in those days. As a final-year boy I felt a little more responsible, even though I was never made a prefect. I received the post of visual aids monitor, which required me to fetch the school film projector. This was a fairly substantial size piece of equipment – and it was kept in the girls' school, which was a great bonus. I would bring the projector back to the class that was showing the film, and with my assistant – yes, I had an assistant – I would set it up, feed the film through the projector ready for the master's instructions, run the film, then afterwards return it to where it was kept.

Every Friday afternoon we were given the choice to attend a class on a subject that we enjoyed. I chose the science lab. I was interested in messing about with old radios. You could buy small books that gave instructions on how to make what was then called a 'wireless set' – it was a popular hobby at the time. I decided to build a crystal set – and I mean build it from scratch: there were no kits in those days. You had to buy your own copper wire of a certain thickness, then wind it so many turns onto an old toilet roll. To make part of the tuned circuit, you would need a 'cat's whisker' along with other small components. For an aerial I would bring from home my own long length of copper wire which I would string outside the science lab on outside drainpipes. Then I would go back in to work on the bench constructing the set, getting it working. Each week, I would make small changes to make the set perform better.

It was great fun. I remember the first time I had it to work, all the boys came over and crowded round, all having a listen on the headset. I was chuffed in these lessons as I thought I was the bee's knees. I was not aware at the time that building this crystal set was to stand me in good stead for getting my first job.

As a younger boy, I had always wanted to be an engine driver. I looked at all the books about engine drivers and how the engines worked. I would go to the engine sheds at Hitchin. I was a keen train spotter; I would buy or be given as a present the Ian Allan pocket books which were updated and published annually. All train spotters had them. I still have some of mine.

The school took the fourth form on visits to the sort of businesses that might employ and train us. I remember visiting a flour mill – I was interested in the workings of the mill. We had a visit to Sainsbury's on Luton High Street – it was swanky and very clean inside: this was where the well-heeled customers bought their goods. I wasn't interested in retail, but fascinated by how things worked, especially an egg checker, which you could shine through the egg to see if it was bad or not.

We also made a visit to Luton Airport, which was nothing like it is today. The boys all went to the English Electric Building on the site. The moment I walked in, I thought, 'Wow, this is where I want to work!'

Around us everywhere there were all sorts of technical gadgets. Someone from the firm asked if anyone was interested in working with them, and as I shot my hand up they noted my name and address. In due course a letter arrived offering me an interview. I went and attended the interview, the first I had ever had. They said they would write to let me know the result.

They did, but, sadly, to say 'no'. Two boys in my class were offered jobs. One, by the name of Taylor, a quiet fair-haired boy who always dressed smartly, lived in a private house. I was disappointed but I congratulated him on taking the position and wished him well: he deserved it.

I had a new ambition, anyway. I wanted to become a television engineer. Television was the technology of the future. Outside of school I began to focus all my time in looking for a job in this industry. I spotted an ad one day in the local paper: Murphy Radio of Welwyn Garden City were looking for young apprentices. I wrote off for an application form, which I filled in and returned. Murphy asked me to visit them for an interview.

When the day came, I was excited and apprehensive: they were asking little old me to go to their factory in Welwyn Garden City for an interview. I travelled alone to get there, and on arrival was shown into a room along with other lads who were all waiting to be interviewed and chatting amongst ourselves. It appeared that I was up against grammar and technical School boys. I was not feeling so good now and started to go into my shell. At last I was called for. They asked me why I wanted the job, and I told them with honest passion about my building of crystal sets and improving their performance. By the end of the interview I felt a little better, but still travelled home thinking I wouldn't get one of those positions with all those grammar boys applying. My dad asked me how the interview went; I said 'alright' and forgot about it.

About a week later I received a letter from Murphy. I got the job. I was elated.

However, this was the start of a battle. My father said it was too far to travel and that I would not keep it up. Now, I see he had a point: in the morning I would have had to get up early, cycle 2 miles to Luton station then catch a train to Welwyn Garden City about 30 miles away. At the time, I was not having any of this. I was determined to go.

He got the headmaster involved and arranged a meeting with Mr Dawes in his school office. The two of them moved heaven and earth to get me to change my mind but I wasn't budging. What I did agree was that if I could find a job in Luton learning how to become a television engineer, I would turn the job down. That was the end of the meeting. I don't think they were too pleased.

I began to scour Luton's television shops to look for a position. In those days there were large numbers of such shops – it was a new, booming market – and they all employed their own engineers. Top of my list of places to work was Coventry Radio. Unlike most other TV shops, which would put televisions in their windows, Coventry Radio would display radio and television components. It was the shop where all the amateur radio constructors went.

Several days after the meeting with Mr Dawes, I had my first lucky break (although I believe you make your own luck in life – a lot, anyway). Walking home from school with a friend, we were passing the headmaster's house. Parked outside it was a Coventry Radio van. I said, 'Let's wait until the man comes out.' Several minutes later, he did, wearing a white coat and carrying a tool box. He was an engineer. Even now, I remember the exact words I said to him: 'Excuse me, mister, is your firm looking for boys to train?'

He was pleasant and helpful, replying that he thought so but that I would have to go in and ask Mr Gordon, the owner. I waited until Saturday morning, made myself look as tidy as possible, travelled in to Luton, had a quick glance into the window of Coventry Radio, took a deep breath and went inside. I had never been inside before. It was awesome.

There were people being served at the counter, so I waited, then someone came over to me to ask what I wanted. I gave him my name and asked if I could speak to Mr Gordon, adding that Colin, the engineer I met had said he would let him know I was coming. Mr Gordon came through from the back of the shop, with a smile – he also had a glass eye that caused him to look at you in a funny way. We went through the back into his office. Trying to make me feel at ease, he invited me to sit down in a chair opposite him, with no desk between us, and asked me to tell him why I wanted the job. I gave him my reasons, saying what I had been doing with crystal sets and not forgetting to mention I had been offered a job training at Murphy's. He offered me the job there and then and said I could start the day I left school, starting on two pounds a week. Without hesitation I said yes; he shook hands with me, and I remember walking back through the shop so proud. I went back home and told my dad. He was happy, too.

It was now almost at the end of my final year. I couldn't wait to leave school. There was a final assembly in the big hall. Mr Dawes went through the list of boys leaving at the end of term by name. He said a little on each boy and what he was going to do when he left, and gave us each a blue-coloured bound book with a leather-type finish, showing our record of each year's exam results. I felt so proud when he called my name and announced I was going to train to be a television engineer.

The school had done a great job. It had helped almost all the boys find a job: some were going into the building trade to learn to be bricklayers or plasterers, some were off to work at places like English Electric. The school was just right for a boy like me, and what I learnt there was to stand me in good stead for the rest of my life. I look back at the dedicated, committed and fantastic teachers, thank them and head into the adult world with fond memories.

Chapter Four

Heartbroken

Such was my life in the public world of school and making my leap into the world of employment. I had another life, however, at 'home'. Here things were much less clear and much harder to deal with.

As I said earlier, my arrival in the household of my father and stepmother propelled us up the council's housing list, and we found ourselves with a fine new home, 43 Yeovil Road. It was part of a new-build council estate between Stopsley and Luton airport, with 500 homes on it. Of the buildings, 90% were what we called 'tin houses', prefabricated, made of mostly tin sheeting and built to last around 20 years (last time I looked, they were still there!). Ours was grander, a steel house. Inside, the design was super and modern: two decent size double bedrooms and a box room enough for a single bed, a nice size bathroom with all modern amenities built in; downstairs a good size airy hallway, a big lounge with a built-in open fireplace behind which was a boiler which supplied the hot water for the central heating of the whole house. There was a dining room and a modern fitted kitchen with a full complement of cupboards, a Heatrae boiler that supplied in a second all the hot water you could ever want, a large outside coal house and a decent-sized garden.

However, none of this matters if the people in it aren't happy. If I can pick out one incident as an example it was one Boxing Day. Usually, I travelled down (on my own) to Abertillery to spend the Christmas period with my mother and sisters, but for some reason I can't recall, it was decided that I was to stay at Luton. I was not very happy about this and moped about the house. Finally this boiled over and I had an altercation with my stepmother. She grabbed out of my hand the Christmas present that my mother had sent me – a German-made Bakelite film projector which came with strips of 35mm film about a foot long which could be fed into the projector and shown on a wall – and threw it into our open hearth fire. I instantly stood up and without thinking put my hand into the fire to salvage it, which I succeeded in doing, though some of the films were ruined.

I could be unpleasant, too. Walking home from Stopsley Park, where my father had been coaching my stepsister in athletics (I was taken along to watch), he and I had an argument about his favouring his children over me. At the high point of this, I turned round to him and said I would rather have Jack Hughes as my father. How cruel children can be. It must have hurt him immensely. But I often felt that I was a hindrance to him in his attempt at a new life. He always repeatedly said to me that when I was older I would understand. I learnt, a lot later in life, that he still had a father's love for me.

There were bright moments. I remember one summer's day, my stepmother packed me up some sandwiches, gave me a bottle of pop and I cycled off to London. I loved my bike, a Rally Trent Sports in green, with drop handlebars, a huge saddlebag and Sturmey Archer gears. It was the best friend I had at that time. I rode down to the Old Oak Common railway sheds in Willesden, and crawled in through a fence when no one was looking. I met some fellow rail spotters from Luton who had cycled up like me, and they asked me if I wanted to join them in going to Camden Town sheds. We did, getting into the premises the same way as we did to Old Oak Common.

We then rode home – a round trip, according to my cyclometer, of around 100 miles. We were all tired on the way back, so we split up. I got a puncture at the foot of the big hill that leads up into Luton. I was pretty well all in by then, but I had to fix it. Everyone carried puncture kits at that time: I got mine out, removed the inner tube, pumped it up to locate the puncture, used a bit of spit on sand paper to rub it down, put a patch on, added a little French chalk, reassembled the wheel – and I was off again. Job done. I arrived home late and absolutely on my knees, but I had had a day of simple pleasure that I will never forget. Even better, I never told anyone at home where I'd been or what I'd completed, so it was my secret.

There was a shop on Stopsley high street which was a stockist for Hornby Dublo trains and accessories. The man who owned the shop ran a club whereby you could pay on the card as much as you wanted, then when you had paid for the item you wanted he would let you have it. I would press my head against his shop window and look at all the little engines, carriages and trucks. Most of the items were beyond my budget, but there was a coal truck I took a fancy to. It cost 4 shillings and sixpence (23p in today's money: a fortune then). I went in and explained what I wanted, and he gave me one of his cards. He knew I didn't have very much, but kept the truck back for me. When I finally got it, I took it home and treasured it, for it was mine and nobody else's.

My dad's brother uncle Cliff came to live with us. He was the youngest of my father's five brothers, a very slim, tall person who walked with a limp due to his having fallen off a ladder in Abertillery. My father arranged for him to take a job as a driver for one of his taxis. When he first came to live with us I shared a bedroom and a double bed with him: I remember getting up in the mornings; there was always a dash for the bathroom. He was a fantastic support for me, kind and considerate. He stayed in the background and didn't get involved in any family tenseness or squabbling; he knew my father's new wife had a temper on her. Every week on a Saturday he would give me a sixpence (for those that weren't around in that time, that equates to two and a half pence in today's money – but was worth a lot then). I treasured those sixpences for it was all I had then. If my uncle Cliff forgot one week, I pride myself that I would never ask him for it as I was not entitled to it – it was a gift, but he wouldn't forget. The next week he would give me two. As I write this even now it brings tears to my eyes.

Cliff was a keen record collector and on the weekends he would play his records. He loved Italian opera singers such as Mario Lanza. I can see him there now, polishing away, cleaning his records. On Sundays, he, my dad and I would play table tennis after lunch on the dining room table – it made a good tennis table with its leaves pulled out at each end and a net set across the middle. I would draw up a league table where we all had to play each other twice.

I also remember the times when an ice cream man came round, which they often did on a council estate. More often than not he would stop right outside our house and play his jingles on his loud speaker. Everyone went out for ice creams, including my stepmother – but she came back with three ice creams for her three children, but none for me. She would say something like, 'Oh, I didn't see you there – but it's too late now; he's gone.' I just kept quiet and accepted it as part of life.

My aunty Silvia was the youngest of my mother's sisters (of which there were four: no boys). She was about nine years older than me and very bright. She went to the county grammar school just outside Abertillery at Nantiglow. When she passed her O levels, her father, a very strict but straight man – remember he was an underground pit manager, and as such had to command respect – wanted her to leave school and find an office job. Her headmaster took time out to visit her father and pleaded with him to let her stay on to take her A levels. It was a happy ending: she stayed on, and the headmaster found her a job with the Met Office where she met and married my uncle Cliff (another Cliff!), a Cambridge graduate. They both moved to Dunstable – just down the road from us – where the Office had a branch.

My aunt came to visit me one Saturday at Yeovil Road. Having no car, she came by bus. Sadly, she did not come often: after a few visits, she had a bust-up with my father, who accused her of trying to steal my affection, and departed the house with tears in her eyes, never to visit it again.

However, she had a stern resolve and would telephone me – as luck would have it, we were one of the few people on the estate who had a phone – and would arrange to meet me on a Saturday afternoon. I would dress up as smart as I could and meet her in Luton. I loved those times with her and always longed for the next one. She would take me into a shop and buy me an item – I especially remember her buying me a tie to commemorate the Queen's coronation in June 1953. It was blue with a bright red pattern: at the time I thought I was the bee's knees wearing it. We would look to see what was on at the picture houses; if there was something we fancied, she'd buy a box of Maltesers to share. After the film my aunt would see me to the bus for my sad return home. I look back now and am moved by the tremendous effort she made for little old me.

She and Cliff moved out of the hostel they were staying in to a rented house at the village of Totternhoe, at the foot of Dunstable downs. It had an extensive view of fields all around and a bus stop outside. I scorned the bus, and would cycle there on my trusty bike for Sunday lunch. Silvia was a great cook. She always made me so at ease in her home: I loved the cleanliness, the lovely soft carpets and soft furnishings. Cliff, a reserved, quiet man would generally be in the background. He would lay the dinner table, and I would be expected to help. I was learning all the time about a different culture, far from mine. We would all talk in the lounge after lunch and continue until tea time, when my aunt would always produce some stunning, juicy, creamy, succulent cakes. On warm days, one could also look out of the windows at the back of the house and watch the gliders gracefully floating to and fro off the thermals coming off the side of the downs: it was all so peaceful that you could almost go to sleep watching them.

I especially remember one beautiful summer's day, when she and I had arranged to go on a long cycle ride. I rode over to the house without a care in the world other than a little excitement about where we were going. When I arrived, a picnic basket was packed up ready to go. We cycled down quiet side roads and tree-lined lanes to Ashridge Park, where we found a beautiful grassy spot to have our picnic with the strong sun beating down on us. After that, we went home. I think Silvia was quite exhausted by the ride, but she seemed very happy. I certainly was.

Back home, my father was a gambler. However he did not let the gambling control him. He became involved in greyhound racing, and owned a greyhound which someone would train for him. At the time, Luton had a greyhound track at Skimpot Lane (it closed in 1973). I remember him coming home one night with a fist full of the old, very large five pound notes. He had won four hundred pounds. He decided to move off the council estate and buy a far better house in a more salubrious part of Luton. The semi-detached house they bought cost about £2,000, which will give you the idea of the value of the £400 he won. The house was near the end of a side road opposite the Luton and Dunstable hospital, with a large back garden (part of which was at the side, wide enough to build another house), neat and tidy lawns and, the bit I thought the best, a large lean-to shed running almost the whole length of the side. My father was not a very practical person when it came to making things, and said I could have the shed as my own. I couldn't wait to move in and carry on making things such as the Keil Kraft balsawood aircraft kits. Beyond the house were open fields, and a footpath cut through to a field and, beyond it, the open downs.

A number of boys from school joined the Boys Brigade, and I did the same. They had a band and a uniform. You supplied your own blazer and grey flannel trousers; they supplied you with a smashing leather belt with a white lanyard to wear diagonally across and around the chest bearing a purse, and a smart forage hat. I felt that this would give me some pride, which I lacked at the time, given the situation at home. It was something to belong to.

I also wanted to learn a musical instrument. What I really wanted was to play the drum, but those slots were all taken, so I ended up learning the bugle. Luckily for me, they had also just set up an arts and craft section. The instructor was a humourless retired old man and his approach was pretty unimaginative: we all had to make the same thing in the same way and at the same pace as he set. But it was nice to make things, and he would never tell us what we were making, which kept us all guessing. I remember one project was a really odd shape, and went on for about six weeks. I didn't have a clue what it was even when it was finished.

There was also drill, standing to attention in military style, tallest on the left, shortest on the right, while Captain Goodwin and his lieutenant would walk around inspecting us thoroughly. We were awarded marks or deductions for our dress and this would go into a league table; the boys always showed a keen interest this, trying to better each other. After inspection we would carry out drill – serious exercises – and then, the bit we enjoyed most, 'O'Grady Says'. This turned drill into a game. Captain Goodwin became O'Grady, and rather than just giving orders, called out something like 'O'Grady says quick march!'. Off we marched. More orders would follow in the same format ('O'Grady says...'). Then he'd slip in an order without the 'O'Grady says', and anyone who followed that order was out. I'm not sure I ever won, but I usually got to the last half-dozen or so, at which point the captain would speed things up and I'd get something wrong. One boy almost always won; he was a lad from the local grammar school who was threatened with expulsion on several occasions. I wouldn't be surprised if he attained success in life, as he was his own man.

There were some super human beings in charge of the Boys Brigade. Captain Goodwin and the lieutenant (who happened to be his brother) knew how our minds worked, but were also very caring. Once, I stopped going to the Brigade after one return from seeing my mother at Abertillery (I was always in an unstable, depressed state of mind after such visits). Captain Goodwin came around my house to enquire why I had stopped going. He had a long chat with my father, then with me, and persuaded me to go back. Mr Tongeman, the local Methodist minister, kept his eye on me, too. He was truly committed to his vocation, and always kind and considerate of others. He would invite me around to his house on Sunday evenings where he had a small group of people gathered to chat. His assistant, a very pleasant lady of around 25 to 30 years of age, particularly took me under her wing.

When I was old enough (I think it was thirteen) I put my name down at the local paper shop, Whitmores on Ashcroft Road. I had words with the boys working there who said it was not easy getting a job with them, but I put my name down on the list anyway and called in on the way to school once a week to ask Mr Whitmore if there were any jobs going yet. I didn't have to wait long before one came up and he gave it to me. The paper round paid half a crown (two shillings and sixpence), delivering every day except Sundays – which had its own waiting list; it paid another half crown just for that one day.

You were expected to turn up by seven in the morning to collect your bag of papers, all marked up with the addresses in delivery order: Mr Whitmore and his son Richard were up at six o'clock to mark them. On five days I had to go home for breakfast then off to school to arrive at nine o'clock for assembly – to be quite honest I thought nothing of it. In time I became a reliable and conscientious paper boy, and eventually Mr Whitmore gave me a Sunday round, which meant I had to get up around six thirty to arrive at the shop before seven to collect my bag of papers. Richard Whitmore was very switched on; you could see he had a smart brain. He went on to become a news broadcaster for the BBC.

Underneath all this, I was sustained by a promise. Mum always promised me that when I left school I could go and live with her back in Wales. I missed her terribly: after visits to her I hated being back with my stepmother, and would spend hours sitting in my little box room and pine, making flying balsa wood aircraft, messing about with electrics or shortwave radios. Every day, I would mark with a red biro a small line on the wall. I would make small groups of lines, from one to six, and every seven days would cross a line through the middle of the latest group, denoting another week gone by towards my next visit to Wales.

In my last year at school, but before I started looking for jobs in Luton, my mother moved to a smarter house, at the foot of a mountain with a playing field opposite. I remember saying to her, 'Mum, I leave school at Christmas. Can I come and live with you, then?' I can't remember the exact words she said, but basically the answer was no. This was after all those years of reaffirming her promise that one day I could live with her. I cried all day. I don't remember being comforted, only ignored. Looking back now I should have known, but at the age I was then you are so green. Her lover boy Hughes didn't want me, and she put him first and always did, not only over me, but also over my sisters. How can someone be so infatuated not to put her children first? After that experience, I thought I would never ever trust anyone again: my heart was broken.

Chapter Five

My First Jobs

Enough of my private life, and off to work!

My first day at Coventry Radio, I was full of enthusiasm and wanted to please everyone. I was taken upstairs by Mr Gordon to the service department which occupied the whole floor of the building, which at one time I suppose was an old house. He introduced me to his service manager, Gordon. During the war he had worked on the early development of radar at RAF Yatesbury, where I would eventually go. He introduced me to the other engineers, Colin, who had got me the introduction, and Terry. I spent my first morning in a loft, sorting a mass of old electrical components. At lunch, we went out to buy fish and chips. After that, Gordon showed me to Terry's room and pointed to a long bench that ran the whole side of one wall. 'This is yours,' he said.

Terry would be my supervisor. He was a friendly person, clear and precise in his speech – he was ex-grammar school. He loved his work, repairing televisions.

I was allowed to attend Luton Technical College for one day a week on a course they were running for radio and television servicing. It was lengthy. In the first three years they would teach radio servicing, after which you took the City and Guilds examination for the qualification as a radio engineer. The second two years took you up to being a fully qualified television service engineer. However it was all theory – we were supposed to be getting the practical input from our employers.

Many of my fellow students were ex-grammar school and found the theory easy. I didn't. Luckily I became friendly with John Barnes, or Barney as we called him. He took me under his wing for maths and physics, and would never scoff at my difficulty with these things but just help me as much as he could. We also enjoyed joking and fooling around – which was eventually to be my downfall...

At work, I learnt a lot from Terry. He would show me the radios that came in for repair, told me what the fault was and how to fix it. I would tell him what I had learnt at the Tec, and he would explain what those things meant in practice. I learnt to use the test gear, including the heavy Mullard Valve Tester that sat at the back of the downstairs showroom. I was given projects such as building Osram 912 amplifiers – high technology at that time. Some of my handiwork ended up on display in the shop window. Terry even invited me to his home to see his workshop where he would take on private repairs. I thought this place was awesome, and told myself I would have one like it one day.

Sometime after I started with the firm, they employed another boy similar to myself with a similar educational background. His name was Bill, and he was a real jokester, fooling about all the time and getting told off. I found myself sucked into this. Bill got the sack, but I carried on where he left off. I became too cocky – and one Friday afternoon Mr Gordon called me into his office and, with real sadness, paid me to the end of the week and sacked me, too.

I could have trained to be a fantastic television engineer working with fantastic people, but instead... I started all over again, looking around Luton for a similar position, but shop owners weren't keen on a lad who had got the sack. The only offer I got was from an owner who I found scary. 'I don't want any f*****g about,' he said with a threatening expression. I went home, thought about it, telephoned him and turned the job down.

Eventually I went to Scrivens in High Town Road. They sold televisions and electrical goods, but their main source of income was electrical contracting for Vauxhall, the motor manufacturer and the biggest employer in the town. When I entered the shop, a tall man approached me asking me what I wanted; I replied that I was looking for a job learning to be a television engineer. He said he was the manager, interviewed me there and then, and offered me a job. I would have to sweep the shop out in the morning, serve customers when he wasn't there, do repairs when he was around, not just of radios but irons, vacuum cleaners or toasters. It was not what I dreamt of, but I was running out of options.

I got on well with the tall man, Mr Wells – I would sometimes accompany him on evening repair jobs. But the shop owner and I disliked each other. I don't really know why, but I still remember the blank look on his face whenever we had any dealings. Another assistant was appointed. Although he was older than me, I had to show him how to do some of the work (and still ended up doing the sweeping in the morning).

One day I was suddenly approached by Mr Wells and told I would be working in the electrical contractors' department somewhere else now. He simply walked away, leaving me to be taken to the Vauxhall factory. I never saw him again.

My boss at Vauxhall was a man named Terry, who was a tough, hard man – but fair-minded. I didn't like the work there, but found the building of cars from scratch fascinating. As the main electrical contractors, we had the freedom to go anywhere in the factory without restrictions, even into the design room where you could see the small wooden models of future products secretly under development. I would watch the cars coming off the assembly line. Then they were building the Cresta, a lovely, sleek-lined car with a very American-type design – lots of chrome everywhere, bright colours and a bull-nose front. These beauties came off the line at the rate of about one every two minutes, where they would be buffed up to look their shiniest and best.

I wanted to get back into radio and television, so one Saturday I went into Fitzroy Radio on the outskirts of town and spoke to the owner, Mr Cardell. I told him what I had been doing since leaving school, and he decided there and then to take me on in his workshop.

The shop looked smart, with televisions spaciously and elegantly displayed in the very clean showroom with no other items to clutter it up. Mr Cardell was a clever entrepreneur who built a grocery business but had now decided that televisions were the product of the future. He did not really know how to service them, however. We made a good team.

On one occasion Mr Cardell had an invitation to visit a small television tube regunning business that had just started up in the area (a regunned tube has had the electronics taken out of the neck and new ones inserted). We were greeted at the door by men in white coats, who enthusiastically showed us how it was all done. They wanted him to buy the regunned tubes, which were about a quarter of the cost of new ones. I knew how tubes were made: at the end of the show-round they asked if we had any questions. Mr Cardell had none, but I asked how they did their gettering (restoring the vacuum in the tube). They mumbled something about not needing it, but I knew the tube wouldn't last six months. Mr Cardell was delighted, as he had just been about to place an order.

Televisions weren't selling as fast as my boss hoped – at that time, there was still only one channel, BBC, in black and white. So he got me doing other pieces of work. Some was with a friend of his, Tom, who erected TV aerials for him. Tom was very safety conscious; I wasn't. He would crawl carefully on ladders; I would walk upright all over slate roofs, thinking I could do anything. Mr Cardell also had me helping him build a 6ft lap wood fence on one side of his garden and then paint it in creosote, before digging a huge hole in his garden – he wanted to build a garage and to have an inspection pit in it.

One day, out of nowhere, Cardell suddenly accused me of wiring a tuner incorrectly and destroying two valves (a lot of tuning work had come in, as a new channel, ITV, was due to come on air) and sacked me on the spot. I was gutted, so I cycled home feeling depressed and thinking I had been dismissed unjustly (unlike my dismissal from Coventry Radio, which I knew had been fair). I told my father and he blew his top, saying that my boss deliberately sacked me as it was my birthday coming up and he would have had to give me a raise.

The following day, I was out looking for a job. I had heard of Blundells, a huge department store slap bang in the centre of Luton (two decades later, it would move to the new Arndale Centre, and shortly after that it would be bought by, and disappear into, Debenhams). It had a television department which was just around the corner from the main store in a large old church they had bought. Once again, I walked in, asked if I could see the manager, had a brief chat with him – his name was Mr Bevan, a jovial-looking man in a dark suit with a large moustache which reminded me of spitfire pilots during the war – and was offered a job there and then.

He took me down to meet the service manager, Jim Pierce – and Jim and I hit it off straight away. He was an ex-national serviceman who served in Egypt for two years in the army, aged around 27, and would become a good friend and mentor of mine. Sometimes Jim would go out on service calls and take me with him: I had a provisional driving licence so Jim would let me use the van with him and he would teach me to drive. He would also talk about his wife – marriage seemed a distant universe for me.

Another of my colleagues was a tall Scotsman who was very much a lady charmer. He would do all the outside service calls, which took him all round the county. There were plenty of rumours that he did more than fix televisions on some of his visits.

Socially, this big organisation was great. It had a social club that organised outings on which I would have a fantastic time. There were plenty of girls of around my age working around the store, especially in the cosmetics department. Work-wise, I was dealing with all sorts of problems, mostly electrical. I say 'mostly' as the new Garrard auto changers on gramophones were supposed to automatically change records stacked on top of each other, but didn't. Customers brought them back thinking it was a complex electrical problem, but actually you needed to bend the mechanism a tiny bit and it then worked. Jim was a dab hand at this – as he was at many things, and taught me a huge amount.

I became an expert on electric razors, another booming post-war consumer goodie. The regional Phillips sales rep arranged for me to go on a one-day course to qualify us to become a regional Phillips shaver centre. The rep met me at St Pancras station, and we travelled down to the Phillips factory at Purley. I spent a very productive day learning how to strip a Phillishaver down to its individual components and rebuilding it again. The Phillips shavers we use today are built almost the same as they were then. When I went in to work the following day, I thought I was the bee's knees, and got a little jovial ribbing about it from the staff. Repairing televisions is a far more difficult accomplishment.

Next to the electrical department was the record department, where two ladies worked: the manager and her assistant, about my age, who was forever coming into the workshop to chat me up. I wasn't very keen on her and would get embarrassed at times trying to ward her off, though we became friends in the end. A carpenter built ten booths in the record department where you could listen to a record before you bought it – Jim and I designed the electronics. Sitting in those booths I was able to tune into the new music that was sweeping the country: Bill Haley was the star, with 'Rock Around the Clock' and 'Shake Rattle and Roll'. Ruby Murray's 'Heartbeat' was another favourite. It was the time of a new, 'teenage' culture. I loved the clothes that went with it, though could rarely afford them, and, fond as I was of my bike, craved a scooter. I had no desire to be a Teddy Boy, however: those lads were clearly trouble.

Not for the first time, I hit my own trouble by not appealing to the owner of the business, a man who lived in Northumberland, where his other store and main office were, and who would drop by every couple of weeks to monitor how things were going. I think he thought I was scruffy (which I guess I was). At one point he told our store manager, Mr Bevan, to get rid of me, but luckily for me, Mr Bevan discussed it with Jim, who hit the roof and pointed out that I earned my weekly wages and more with the valves I returned to Mullard for replacement under guarantee.

When turned 17, I went up to Mr Bevan's office and asked him for a pay rise. He gave it to me without any fuss. I even remember him saying to me: 'Malcolm, you won't go far wrong in life.' It's good when people have faith in you.

I was happy at Blundells, but wanted more adventure. There was an RAF recruitment centre in St Albans, and I travelled down there one Saturday. I had an interview with two corporals. I wanted to be like these men: smart and self-confident. I also had a medical, which I did not pass. My condition, as diagnosed by Dr Franklin, rendered me unsuitable – then. I felt that was that for joining the RAF.

Still, I was happy with my job, with studying at the Tec and with seeing my friends.

At the top of our road, there lived a girl I fancied, doing A levels. Education-wise she was one up on me, but she would go on the same walks as me. One day, quite by accident, we went for the walk at the same time. I plucked up courage and asked her if she would mind me joining her. She looked a little flushed, as I think she knew I liked her, but said yes.

It was a beautiful walk, though we didn't say a lot to each other. When we arrived back at the outside of my house, we said our goodbyes: I never had the courage to ask her out, thinking she would say 'no'. After that I would regularly see her at the end of the road. We would just look at each other. Now I think that if I'd asked her to go to the pictures with me, she would have said yes. I had in my head a fear of attractive young women, planted there by my stepmother. She would ridicule me, as if there was something dirty about sex. One day when she was rattling on about it, I remember my father telling her, 'Leave the boy alone, will you?'

My best mate John Barnes – Barney – brought a lot of fun into my life at this time. He was a good cyclist, and he and I would ride back from technical college together, racing the red double decker buses along the main Dunstable Road. Even in those days, there was a lot of traffic, and we'd often win. He also introduced me to the local youth club. It had a great atmosphere – there was no yob culture, just the chance to have fun. We had great times playing table tennis, and there were plenty of nice girls there to meet and chat to. At other times, I would go to Barney's house. His mum thought the sun shone out of his backside – how unlike my stepmother. He would invite a few friends in and we would play cards for small amounts of money. His mum would make supper for us.

I also took up golf, through a friend of my father's, Archie Fosey. Fossey only had one arm, but still played off a handicap of ten. He invited me to go with him one evening to Dunstable Downs club for a free trial to see if I would enjoy it. Being a charismatic gregarious person, he persuaded the professional Stuart Fields, a plus handicap golfer who played at all the big major events, to join us. Stuart lent me some clubs – all for right-handed players (I was left-handed). But it all went well, and I soon found myself up on the practice field, whacking balls with a set of old clubs that Archie had bought for me. All right-handed, of course. I just had to learn to play that way.

So, in a way, I was adjusting to being unable to live with mum. But fate had another bad thing lined up for me.

Chapter Six

The Transport Café

A friend of my father's, who was an estate agent in Luton, uprooted his life and moved to Devon to establish himself in the profession there. One day, he contacted my father saying there was a golden opportunity for him to buy a transport café at Clyst Honiton, just outside Exeter, on the main London road (remember there were no motorways in those days). The cafe was going for almost a song.

My father asked if I wanted to come with him to look at it, and one morning we took an early train to Exeter. The Black Horse Café had been put up after the war, purpose-built for its intended use, with a good-sized car park. The whole development was cut into the side of a hill consisting of red Devon sand. Inside there was upstairs accommodation with three bedrooms, a living room and all mod cons. The extra commercial twist was that there were 12 guest bedrooms, which we were told were always filled by transport drivers. In the dining area, we met Mr Pope, the owner, and his wife. He looked a very ill man. I had the impression that he loved the business, which he had built up from nothing. On the way back to London, all my dad could talk about was buying the Black Horse Café. Despite his having no experience of the trade, he was adamant he could make a go of it.

He wanted me to work with him in the business, adding that it would be mine one day.

I did not want to. I was very happy working at Blundell's. I was enjoying my studies at the technical college, which were helping me towards my ambition of becoming a good television engineer. I had made good friends in Luton and didn't want to leave them.

But I had little choice. If I rebelled against my father, I'd have to live in digs and I didn't earn enough to pay for digs and the basics of life. So I said my goodbyes to all the good people I knew in Luton. With the exception of my relatives, to this day I have never come across any of them again.

On the day of moving, my father and I travelled down by train early morning to take the keys and stock over. He carried all the money he had in a big wad of notes in his trouser pocket – I think it was just enough to pay for the stock and wages and food delivery up to the end of the week. You have to admire him for believing in himself; he was never one to go to the bank for assistance; he believed in paying his way as you go along. That's how it was in those days for most small businesses.

We got to work straight away and didn't stop till late at night. Next morning we were up early – the café was busy; the cook was making breakfasts as fast as he could; we had lorries filling the car park. Apparently it was like this every morning. My father decided he wanted me at the counter and in control of the till, something I had never done before. It was my first job handling money, and I was slow to pick it up, but I managed.

Later, I was put on night shift, which gave me time during the day (I also had Wednesday off). He paid me £4.00 a week cash, which was generous.

I had disposed of my bike in Luton, so had to take the bus into Exeter. There was a boy's club in Heavitree where you could play snooker and table tennis, but it wasn't like the friendly, mixed Dunstable youth club. Most of the lads were alright, but there were one or two who, when around, it would be best to keep your hand on your wallet.

I loved going into Horne Bros on Exeter High Street and admiring the type of clothes they sold: cavalry twill trousers, beautiful blazers, smart Van Heusen shirts. I also had my eye on a Lambretta scooter. There was a motor cycle shop near the city centre at the top of Paris Street that sold them on hire purchase: once I'd saved the deposit, I bought one, a light cream 150cc. The shop arranged the insurance and gave me a full tank of petrol; I rode off feeling like a big cheese again.

That summer we had glorious weather on the Devon Rivera. My new best friend, Lambretta, and I travelled all over the county. Torquay was a favourite of mine. I would go down to the quay side and just watch the comings and goings – sometimes I felt a certain loneliness, so would ride to a lovely little café where I would have tea and crumpets. At other times, I'd travel into Exmouth where there was a dance hall. Some nice girls would go there; I remember dating one who lived in Exeter. I also met Vic Kier, who lived in Cullompton. He reminded me of Barney and became a good friend. Vic had an old banger of a car, which was his pride and joy. Coming from a poor family, he had to do all his own repairs. He would drive out to the café to see me – my dad was pleased I had made such a good friend – and we would go for a ride in his banger. It often broke down: Vic would say 'Wait a minute', run around the front, lift the bonnet, tinker with a few wires, then say with his normal grin, 'That's OK now', and off we would go again.

So I had money in my pocket, was getting around on my Lambretta and was generally having a good time. Yet deep down, I was not happy with my present situation. I wanted to break away from my stepmother's influence, make my own way in life and fulfil my ambitions. There was an RAF recruitment centre in Exeter, and one day I went quietly in and explained what I wanted to do. I now had my City and Guilds certificate – I had taken the final exams down in Exeter – which would allow me to enter a junior technicians course. The officer in charge said I would have to take a test first, that it would take an hour, that if I wanted I could come back another time to take the test. I said I would rather take it now, and he gave me a quiet room to sit in for the test, which consisted of 100 questions on radio theory. I completed all the questions in the allotted time. The officer told me to wait ten minutes; I did so, nervously; he came back informing me I had passed and would recruit me on a wireless fitters' course. I was asked if I wanted to be a ground or air wireless fitter: for me the answer was a no-brainer, working directly on aircraft had an adventurous feel about it. I was asked how many years

I wanted to sign on for. I had already decided three. The officer said I would have to come back for a medical.

I left still thinking I would fail the medical as before – but when it happened, I kept very quiet and only answered the questions. At the end I was told I'd passed and that I'd be sent a rail ticket for travel to Cardington, where all new RAF personnel except for officers went. You could have knocked me down with a feather duster.

Then I went home and told my father my good news. He did not see it as good news. Instead, he just kept saying 'You'll be back.' I showed no emotion.

I can understand now: I messed all his plans up.

I also told Vic, and he said that, quite unknown to me, he had done the very same thing. He was going in to be a teleprinter operator.

The day came for me to catch the train. My dad said very little, except (again) that I'd be back. I felt no sadness, just excitement. I was breaking the shackles of suppression and starting a new adventurous life for myself. Sitting on the train I had plenty of time to think about all that had happened in the past few weeks – and to worry about one thing; I would have to go through a more thorough medical at Cardington.

CHAPTER SEVEN

STARTING MY LIFE IN THE RAF

Arriving at Cardington station, I stepped off the train with more lads like me, all joining the RAF and looking a little sheepish. Our transport was waiting to drive us to the camp: a large RAF-blue Bedford truck sporting a tin roof with a rope dangling from the middle of the back. The flight sergeant that greeted us said with authority, 'Jump on, lads!' We all helped each other on board, then sat on the benches around the sides of the truck, not saying much and looking at each other rather glumly. On arriving at Cardington camp we were taken straight to our billet consisting of a large wooden shed, with around twenty single beds constructed of sturdy steel tubing with strong wire mesh across it and a mattress 4 or 5 inches thick (very little spring in it). Each bed had a locker to keep your personal items in on one side, and on the other a tall, narrow wardrobe for hanging your clothes in.

As we walked in, a very loud authoritative voice called from behind us: 'Choose any bed you like, lads.' We all scuttled about choosing a bed for ourselves, and at the same time looking to see where the voice came from. Standing in the doorway was a tall upright flight sergeant major, wearing all his war ribbons and sporting a large RAF type moustache, waxed and pointed at the ends. After we had sorted ourselves out and had something to eat, he gave us all a very intimidating talk. Two of the lads packed up and went home next morning (national service had just come to an end; a national service man could never walk out like that). The rest of us would stick it out for the rest of the week, and they would see who they would accept for entry to the RAF.

We became more relaxed and started talking amongst ourselves: the lads with me came from all over the country. During the week we had all sorts of tests to complete; they were finding out our strengths and weaknesses to ensure that what we had elected to do was suitable for each individual.

The one thing that made me nervous now was the medical examination. I knew this was my Achilles heel. The medical centre was crawling with RAF doctors, all specialists in their own fields. I thought, 'Crumbs, I'll never get through this.' When it was time for the heart specialist, as in Exeter I was quiet and said nothing except answering the questions he gave me. I felt he was taking a long time with me, then he stopped and called a colleague over who listened to my heart. They then had a chat amongst themselves, came over to me and asked how long I was in for and what trade I was in for. I emphasised that I was on a wireless fitter's course; they paused for a moment then the senior one said, 'OK, we will pass you.'

Wow! I was on cloud nine, fantastic. It only shows that if you try hard enough you can succeed against all the odds stacked against you.

The final act was to swear on the Bible allegiance to Queen and country.

Before leaving Cardington on a special military train for Bridgnorth, Shropshire, where we were to undertake three months of square bashing, we had to be kitted out with our uniforms. A tailor was present to make the necessary alterations to ensure they would fit properly. We were issued with all we would need: underwear, shirts, socks, shoes, boots, eating implements. The RAF number I had been given – I can remember mine to this day – was stamped on every piece, then it all had to be packed into a kitbag.

The lads were keyed up. It was a long journey, and we had fun playing cards and joking: the lads' individual personalities were starting to uncover themselves, but we all thought that now wearing a blue uniform we were big cheeses. On arriving at Bridgnorth station, instead of being greeted with a truck with a rope hanging down the rear, a bus was waiting.

At the camp (a much more relaxing place than Cardington, which on reflection was more like a prisoner of war camp – a little harsh, I know) we were taken to our billet. It was immaculate. The light brown floor shimmered in a smooth light, almost dazzling in my eyes. The beds were lined up with bed packs on them perfectly made up (a bed pack is when all your sheets and blankets are neatly folded up into one of the blankets, making a small rectangle with the sides and the top looking very square). All the wooden cupboards and wardrobes were in perfect position and gleamed. There were pads on the floor to put your feet in when moving around, which you would do in a sliding motion to keep the floor polished. Outside, all the grass and borders were immaculately kept…

Now who do you think would keep it like this? Yes you're right, the square bashers, us.

In behind us came the corporal who would be in charge of us for the next three months, our drill instructor, Corporal Fellingham. Most of these instructors had a reputation for being really nasty to new recruits, but we were lucky: the corporal was a man who got the best out of people by persuasion not bullying. He could, of course, be tough when he thought it necessary. Coming in behind him was the intimidating-looking flight sergeant, wearing all his war ribbons and a typical large RAF moustache, pointed and waxed at the ends. He was tough, but the times when he had me in his office, he would show a different side: he could be very understanding and considerate. As I later found out, he had a dossier on each recruit and knew a lot more about us than we thought. Now he just said, 'Go to the mess, lads, and have some food.'

We grabbed a pit (bed) each then went to eat, not forgetting to take our KNF (knife, fork, spoon) and large glazed white earthenware mug. On our return, we unpacked then made our pits up from our bed packs. Corporal Fellingham came in, and shouted 'Stand by your beds!' – this was the order that all recruits had to obey when anyone senior came into the billet. The flight sergeant came in; we were shouted to attention and he gave us a talk about all the do's and don'ts and what we would be doing for the next three months before the passing out parade.

We then had to select a person to be in charge of the billet. There was one lad, a Scotsman, a pleasant enough person who had been in the RAF cadets and who appeared to be aware of the tasks we would have to perform such as cleaning our boots (they had raised pimple-like spots all over them and we had to ensure a mirror like image on the toe). We elected him. By now we were all pretty well whacked out. I went to bed happy and contented; my head hit the pillow and the next thing I knew, everyone was getting up.

It was just after the crack of dawn. There was a stampede for the showers and washrooms. I had never shaved before. During our lecture the night before we were instructed to shave every day, but I, thinking I was smart, decided not to bother as there was nothing to shave off. On our inspection before the start of the day, Corporal Fellingham came along the line. He stopped, looked me straight in the eye, and said, 'You haven't shaved. This is your first and last warning. I will be watching you.'

We drilled all morning every morning, then would march off as a squad to the mess for lunch (we had to march everywhere as a squad). I would be hungry and exhausted. After eating, we had the afternoon waiting for us, when we did various things. There was an hour with the chaplain discussing religion: a time we almost all found to be a good one to doze off (he being the chaplain would say nothing). We would study RAF history: I enjoyed this subject. We had PT. RAF instructors in their tight sleeveless skimpy vests with their chests puffed out put us through all the exercises. I was not keen on this and I was knackered on completion.

When the afternoon finished, after going back to the billet we would march together to the evening meal, then back to the billet, having deserved an evening's quiet. Quiet? Oh, no, we had to clean the billet, polish all our brass buckles, buttons and badges, and work on our shoes to obtain that mirror image. This would take hours and hours. If you were given jankers (RAF term for punishment) you would have to do that first – lucky for me this only happened once: I was handed a pair of small scissors to cut the already immaculate lawn outside until whoever was supervising me was satisfied.

The billet also had to elect a recruit to represent them on the mess committee which convened once a month. I drew the short straw, probably because I had worked in the kitchen of my father's café. The lads were always complaining about the food in the mess, so they all piled into me with their complaints, which I duly noted. I went to the first meeting in some big fancy place – it may have been in the officers' quarters. They made us feel relaxed and welcome; it was not a sit down formal meeting, we 'mingled' and were served nice biscuits and tea in bone china by batmen (officers' general dogsbody). I could get quite addicted to this, I thought. I was still very green and naïve – but also, me being the person I am, determinedly pushed for my lads' needs. I felt I was just being fobbed off with excuses, and in no uncertain terms said I thought this was all a farce.

During the following month there was no improvement in the mess, so the lads began blaming me as if it were my fault. I attended the meeting again; the same rituals were gone through. The same thing happened again: 'Thank you for the feedback, we will look into it…'. By this time, I appeared to be getting to them. They could see the look on my face. I was avoiding them and they were avoiding me. I was glad to leave the smooth talking of theirs and arrive back at the billet, where the lads were still blaming me saying I was not standing up for myself. The following month I went again to the meeting – and the same old routine of fobbing off. They and I knew that the next month there would be a new intake, and round the roundabout they'd go again. I learnt a lot from that experience.

Early on in our time square bashing, several of the lads whom I reckoned considered themselves hard men saw me as a pushover and started to bully me. This all happened over about a week and came to a climax one day when I was sitting on my bed. Four of them strolled over, stood around and started to goad me into hitting one of them. I ignored them, but they kept persisting, so I said that there was only one of them who would stand up on his own and fight. They took the bait and started to cross-examine me to find out who it was, suddenly keen to know who I thought was the brave one. I expect they were thinking, 'I hope it's me.' But I wasn't telling. In the meantime all the other lads in the billet were watching in silence. I reckoned I was on my own, then all of a sudden one lad about three beds down from me jumped up. He was a quiet lad but very religious. He came down to my bed and said in no uncertain tone, 'Leave him alone or you will have to deal with me.' I think the four others were shocked more into embarrassment than afraid, and crept off to their beds.

I never thanked the lad that came to my help or talked about it with him or anyone else. Why, I don't know. It suppose it was my pride; I never asked for help and felt I didn't need it. Looking back now I should have thanked him and perhaps stood up for myself and smashed my fist into the most aggressive one's nose.

The lads in our flight were all basically good people, including the four that were bullying me. To give an example, every morning the mail would be delivered in one batch then handed out in the billet. As soon as the lads saw the mail they would all stop whatever they were doing and make a beeline for it. Most would receive mail on a daily basis then go quietly to their bed space, sit down and read the letter in private. I never expected any mail; I would stay on my bed. This never bothered me. The lads must have noticed this; most never spoke about it, but several – including the bully boys – quietly approached when I was alone, and with sympathy asked me why I never received any mail. I spoke the truth and left it at that. I felt from then on that they were always behind me and understood.

One afternoon our flight was taken to the firing range. We all thought this would be super fun. Some lads were saying how they had fired rifles before, passing on information that they considered would be useful to those of us who had never fired them. We were called onto the range in batches of ten, as there were ten firing slots. Each had a round target about a yard in diameter, 100 yards away. Right in the centre was a half black, half white circle, about two inches in diameter. We were informed that if you hit this small circle, it was equivalent to hitting a man at 200 yards.

I was given a .22 bore rifle and five bullets, then put myself into the lying down position. I was careful in my shooting and slow; most of the ten finished well before me. If you hit the target, a black dot would show up where the bullet went through, but every time I fired no black dot would show up. The lads noticed this and started to laugh at me. I was starting to feel a right Charlie, but persevered with the same routine, as I was sure I was doing it right. When all the bullets had been fired, I felt a little red-faced, as by this time the lads were in stitches with laughter at me. The instructor told to us to collect our targets for him to mark. When I collected mine, I saw all my shots had gone through the black part of the centre with each hole cutting into one another.

'What a brilliant shot you are,' the lads said. It made me feel chuffed, but we hadn't finished yet. The RAF presented marksman's badges to top riflemen, made of fabric with the shape of two crossed rifles, to be worn on the sleeve of your arm. All us AC 'plonks' (RAF term for Aircraftsman 2, the lowest rank in the service) fancied having a badge on their arm. We could qualify for one on this exercise, but had to use a .303 rifle. The instructor handed me one, telling me to keep the butt very tight to my shoulder, for if I didn't, the kick from the firing could break my collarbone.

I received five rounds of ammo to line the sights up to suit my eyes. I had to shoot for the centre of the bullseye with my first shot, note where the bullet entered, adjust the sights, then shoot again, repeating this until all five bullets were used. I lay down on the ground in the firing position – the instructor told me to spread my legs apart as it helped take the recoil. I did this, and fired. The recoil knocked my whole body back about four inches.

Once I had sorted the sights, I was then handed a further five rounds to shoot for my marksman badge. I told myself to be cool and take my time, but with each shot my aim became shakier. I was happy when it was finished. We then had to fire a Bren gun, a type of machine gun which required two men, one to fire it and another to load the next magazine. I thought this was easy. Some of the lads thought they were John Wayne or Audie Murphy in the Second World War films, firing the whole magazine of 32 rounds in one blast, spraying bullets everywhere except where they were supposed to. They obviously forgot, conveniently or otherwise, that we were instructed to squeeze the trigger in short bursts firing three or four rounds at a time.

At the end of all this, despite my dislike of the .303, I got my marksman's badge.

The parade ground was the central focus of our time at Bridgnorth. The squad would spend two hours after breakfast each week day bashing around it, from the day after we arrived to the passing out parade at the end of our three months training. Like many of us, I had never been on a parade ground before (some of us had been in the RAF cadet force). We began by simply learning to march. It was a shambles on the first day, but by the end of the first week Corporal Fellingham had knocked us into shape. This included teaching us how to form a squad, which ensured that all the airmen's heights matched to form a smooth-looking group. In the second week, he started to look for a marker – that's the one who marches at the front corner of the squad, from whom everyone takes their lead. If he makes a mistake such as turning left when the order was to turn right, the whole flight becomes a shambles. If he goes out of step, the whole squad has to change step to get in step with him: not exactly a pretty sight. Normally the marker is one of the taller airmen. As I was almost six feet, he decided to try me. I didn't mind:and thought of the Boys Brigade where we would march in the big school when we played O'Grady. I was conscious that the whole flight was relying on me. To let them down was the last thing I wanted. Sadly, I couldn't take the pressure and made mistakes. I couldn't maintain my concentration for two hours; somewhere along the way I had lapses. It was like the Boys Brigade, where I was good at O'Grady but there was always this boy that won because he had superb concentration. That was the end of my marking career.

Soon we were all marching perfectly in unison. It gave a sense of pride, of bonding, of comradeship. Next came a time we had all been looking forward to: the issuing of rifles. We were all given our own one which we were individually responsible for. In our billet, fastened onto a wall, was a rifle rack onto which all rifles were placed, minus the bolt. Exactly made for each rifle, this had to be put in our lockers for safe keeping. The rifles were from World War Two – and they were heavy! We had to look after them, of course. We learnt how to clean the inside using four by two cloth, which you pull through the barrel to clean it. There would be gun inspection in the billet; our instructor would look down the barrel to see if it was clean. If it wasn't, you would receive a b****cking.

The first day on the parade ground with our rifles we did very little marching. We were taught how to shoulder them and to bring them to the attention position. Once we were all marching smartly with them, we were introduced to the bayonets, which we then carried fixed onto the end of the rifle barrel. (We weren't issued with the blade type of bayonet, essentially a knife, but a spike, known as the 'pig sticker'. They wouldn't trust us with a blade, which was wise. Even with the pig sticker there were several accidents, but no cuts.)

One day, we all had inoculations before going on parade. The one for tetanus proved the worst, as it causes you to have a stiff arm: painful in itself, but to go on the parade ground straight afterwards… Corporal Fellingham persuaded us it was best to keep our arms moving; we accepted, apart from one or two grumbles. It was very painful and we were very glad when midday came. I remember being sat with some of the other lads around a mess table, talking about injections and blood, when a mate next to me fainted, sticking his face into his dinner. However a couple of days later, we were back to normal.

The squad carried on improving. We thought we were the bee's knees, brilliant at drill with a rifle and fixed bayonets. One or two of the lads mastered the Queen Anne salute, a manoeuvre that involves swirling the rifle around at speed.

The day came for our passing out parade, to which family would be invited. I and all the lads were excited. It was a beautiful sunny day, and the parade ground had been set out for the occasion, with space for the invited guests of two hundred young airmen. The lads of my squad found out, I don't know how, that no one from my family was going to attend. I wasn't bothered by this, as it was a normal occurrence for me. But we had a Scotsman from the Gorbals who had a big heart which he wore on his sleeve. All his family were coming, including his sister. He wanted me to take her out that evening. It was a heartfelt gesture – but I felt offended by it, and told him so. (He didn't give up, however, and after the parade introduced me to her, a pleasant looking girl. I apologised but had already given my answer. Such was the camaraderie we had built up, there were no hard feelings.)

The squad formed up outside the billet and marched proudly to the parade square, puffing our chests out with pride for all to see. Once in position we were stood down. The commanding officer appeared and the whole square was brought to attention for the inspection. This was completed, successfully without mishap, then came the march past in front of the commanding officer. The traditional 'eyes right' was carried out by each flight as it passed. The RAF band played good marching tunes, which were a big help to all keeping us together as one. Finally, the parade came to a close with all flights marching off to the music. After marching back to our billet we were dismissed, all so elated that we couldn't stop gabbing away to each other.

We were then released for lunch and told to reassemble after it, when we would receive our postings. I already knew where my posting was, as only one camp trained wireless fitters: number two radio school, RAF Yatesbury. The flight sergeant major gave a speech complimenting us on our achievements, then handed out the postings. When he came to me, he said you have done well to have that posting. I remember him to this day saying that: quietly, it meant a lot to me.

We were given one week's leave with a train pass to our home and a return pass from home, in my case to Calne station only several miles from Yatesbury camp. The following morning we said our goodbyes and dispersed to our homes all around Britain. Sadly, none of the lads of the flight ever crossed my path again.

My train pass was unfortunately for Exeter, so that's where I went, not knowing the reception that might be in for me. I caught a bus to the café, entering through the side door of the kitchen dressed in my uniform. All the staff I knew welcomed me with glee, asking all sorts of questions. My father came in. I said, 'Hello dad'. He didn't have a lot to say, although he was respectful. I remembered his last words to me when I had left for the RAF: 'You'll be back', meaning 'I hope you will fail the medical.'

During my absence, they had acquired a caravan and placed it in the field behind their flat to use as an extra bedroom for any private guests. My father said I could use it, which suited me down to the ground. The caravan was comfortable and cosy inside, but best of all my stepmother and I were kept apart. My best friend Lambretta was still there to welcome me, and during my week's leave I was to have some great fun with it. I think my father was hoping (although he never asked) that I would help him in the café during the week, but there was no chance. I was on holiday.

My leave coincided with scorching weather. I loved driving my Lambretta to Torquay, as before sitting down by the harbour and peacefully enjoying the graceful sight of fishermen and their trawlers and the suntanned holiday makers, then slowly making my way over to my little favourite restaurant. I would order my tea and crumpets: for me they were the best. I was on cloud nine, a happy, free man. In the evening, it was time to head to the dance hall in Exmouth, the place to be for all the young folk in their prime to have a simply smashing time.

Then my week's leave came to an end; I packed my RAF bag up and caught the train to the next chapter in my life.

CHAPTER EIGHT

YATESBURY

RAF Yatesbury is situated directly alongside the main A4 London road, in flat green, open countryside. I entered via a huge barrier, reported to the guard room and showed my identity card (in RAF language a 1250) for clearance. My accommodation would be hut X4, a super location, the fourth hut from the guard room and alongside the A4. Hut X4 was a typical RAF wooden billet with beds and furniture lined up as the norm, but with one exception: the absence of gleaming polish. There were no floor pads to put on our feet. A number of lads had arrived before me and had already grabbed pit spaces. I followed suit, then we all had a chat, finding out about each other. Most were SACs (senior aircraftmen), the rest like me, 'direct entrants' who had achieved the criteria for entry onto a wireless fitters' course at an RAF recruitment centre. I walked to the mess with some of the lads in a casual way, had a good nosh, and returned to the billet to see it had become much fuller, with more lads having arrived. Most would be on the wireless fitters' course like myself.

Monday morning, we had to report to a classroom hut. We were given a course number, AWF 156 (the 156th wireless fitters' course to be given at Yatesbury). The first three months of it were taken by a national service man with a degree in mathematics from Cambridge. He was short and nervous, and the lads would rag him to bits. He had no idea how to handle men. I was sometimes embarrassed for him, as he was a nice guy. He taught us radio theory and physics, but put it over as if we were Cambridge undergraduates. We had no idea what he was talking about. We had tests every several weeks and almost all, including me, would fail. Those that failed could be 'back classed' to the next entry coming a month behind us, or, in extreme cases, thrown off the course, so pressure was on us. At the end of the three months, almost all of the class were in a position where they could be back classed, but no one wanted this as it would disrupt the whole system. So several SACs were sent back to their units as not being up to it but the rest of us were passed. I was very pleased to put that part of the course behind me.

We now changed to a different classroom for the next phase, radio technical theory. Our instructor was a Mr McClelland, a civilian and one of their top notch men. He stood no nonsense from anyone and could handle trouble with ease.

Meanwhile, out of the classroom, my old mate from Exeter, Vic Kier, having signed up to become a teleprinter operator, began his course just down the road at RAF Compton Bassett. Knowing that I was at Yatesbury, he came to visit, not only to visit an old mate but also looking for a lift home to Exeter. I had not been back to Exeter since arriving at Yatesbury. After my chat with Vic I decided to go back there to collect my best friend, Lambretta. As an AC2 signed up for three years, I was short of money, so I decided to don my uniform to thumb a lift on the next weekend. Wearing my uniform it was easy. I arrived at the café unexpected, stayed the weekend then travelled back to camp on my trusted scooter. Thereafter on many weeks, Vic and I would travel to Exeter and back via Bristol – several times in the pouring rain. I'd arrive back at the camp absolutely drenched, even with the fairing I had on the scooter.

I was having a whale of a time. It did have negatives. I disliked the scruffiness of our billet; the floor was always a mess with rubbish over it. Some people brought their motor bikes in for servicing; there was clothing strung all over some people's bed space. There was the inevitable bully, but I soon saw him off. On sports afternoon we were allowed to take part in any sport of our choosing. I decided along with several of my friends to go to judo lessons, because they were easy to get to, taking place two huts away from us. There was a good standard with several black belts. We first learnt how to fall correctly, then the basic throws. One day, back at the billet, the bully came up to me looking for a fight. He grabbed the front of my uniform, in the middle of the room where everyone could see. Remembering my judo, I used his weight to pull him towards me then stepped forward, put my leg behind his and used his own weight to make him fall over. I stood over him, looked him straight in the face and said nothing. He slunk off and never bothered me again.

Positives were plentiful inside or outside the camp. The camp NAAFI (Navy, Army, Air Force Institute) was on the doorstep. Music from the juke box came floating out the door with all the latest pop tunes of the late 1950s, I recall one called 'Patricia' – my wife, whom I was yet to meet. Ruby Murray ('Lipstick on my Collar') visited the camp to perform. There was also the NAFFI club in Chippenham. I would go there with friends from Yatesbury; most of the lads in the club were RAF. The main feature of the club was the dance hall, and best of all, the area's female talent were there. They all had to be vetted by the manager as suitable: any misbehaving and their pass would be taken away. I will say no more.

There was a great coffee bar on Chippenham High Street, The Salamander, where airmen could any time of day congregate with the local girls. On the weekends I would travel on my Lambretta all over Wiltshire. I went to Stonehenge, which in those days was not surrounded by fencing. I could visit it with friends, with only the occasional other person about, and imagine how it would have looked in the Stone Age. The Amesbury Circle was just down the road, near a pub used by many Yatesbury airmen.

Sometimes we would gamble, playing cards all through the night. One occasion after playing cards until way beyond midnight, around eight of us decided to go to a well-known all night transport café on the A4 the other side of Marlborough, around fourteen miles away. We entered the place all hungry and ordered a typical transport meal – when who should I bump into but my father's eldest brother, Uncle Billy. A bit simple in his intellect and scruffy looking, he peered at me with a serious look, then said: 'What are you doing here at this time of night? It's not safe you know.' As one of eight young, fit airmen, I didn't know what to say to that. It didn't take long with the bush telegraph to get back to my father, who gave me a flea in my ear for it.

We carried on in the classroom with Mr McClelland teaching us radio theory along with the practical side of understanding the pieces of equipment that we would be servicing. There would be five on an aircraft: the VHF transmitter receiver, the radio compass, the Instrument Landing System (ILS), the SSR18 transmitter receiver and the AYF radio altimeter. There would be a practical test on the piece of equipment taught at the time, requiring us to find a number of faults the examiner had cleverly placed in it. We had one hour to find all of them; we were marked at the finish, and this would go towards the final total at the end of the course. I shone out on all these tests, very often getting top marks and being first to finish; my old job in civvy street was a great help to me.

Before we leave Yatesbury, I must write about two unfortunate experiences I had with motor bikes. One evening I persuaded a friend to lend me a 350cc Triumph with a fairing as I wanted to go into Bath. On the return trip – it was a warm night and the road surface was dry – I was driving at a normal speed up the well-known Box Hill, when completely out of the blue, a cow shot out from the left hand side. The front of the bike hit its head and neck smack square on. I was catapulted into the air in a forward motion. I could see I was going to land on the grass verge (my headlight was still on), so tucked my head under my chin, held my left arm out and made it into a curve to complete a forward roll – as I had learnt in judo. I stood straight up, with no injuries or cuts and not even dazed. The bike looked in a pretty bad state, with the fairing hanging off with cow's blood on. It was just about drivable, so I drove it carefully back to camp.

As if not satisfied with one motor bike indent, one Sunday afternoon, the weather being warm and hot, the lads were hanging around the billet. One of them owned a big 500cc Triumph. We were all having a turn at riding it, turning right out along the A4, then turning round and pushing the speed up as far as you could, so the lads could see you speed past the camp gates (on a long straight stretch of road). It came to my turn. To think back now it was crazy: I was wearing a pair of trousers, a summer short-sleeved shirt, and I had no crash helmet on. I had never ridden a bike as big as this before. It was heavy at slow speed and not easy to handle. I got to the turning point and started the run past the camp gates. A light touch on the throttle made the bike accelerate powerfully; I glanced at the large speedometer and wondered 'can I push it to 100mph?'

The answer was 'yes'. The moment the needle touched 100, I braked. This caused the bike to wobble violently. For a moment I felt I had lost control. However, I just managed to keep it upright. I hate to imagine what would have happened to me coming off at 100mph, dressed as I was.

On my holiday leave I would make for Wales on my Lambretta to spend time with my mother and sisters. However, I was faced with the problem of Jack Hughes, her lover who split up the marriage to my father. Hughes' own sister always said he was a waster, a womaniser, and her husband Owen had no time for him. But Jack and my mother were now married.

On my first trip to Wales from Yatesbury, I made for Abertillery, where I thought they were living, only to discover that they had moved away. I drove to my grandmother's house where my father had been brought up. She welcomed me in. Lucky for me, one of her sons, my uncle Ray, was a conductor on the buses. He always knew what was going on in the community and discovered that my mother and Jack had become tenants of a public house in Pontypool.

I made a number of visits. At this time the two Severn bridges weren't built: the quickest and best way to Wales was to cross the Severn via the ferry that operated from Aust on the English side and Beachley on the Welsh side, saving me a sixty mile, two-and-a-half-hour journey via Gloucester. I would load the Lambretta onto the Severn King or Severn Queen for the 15 minutes' crossing. Getting the bike on and off was always a hazardous exercise; on one occasion I almost lost it to the river.

Later, my mother and sisters moved with Hughes to the Severn Tunnel Working Man's Club – yet again nobody had informed me.

On one visit there, I discovered that my elder sister, Margaret, had married, with a white wedding, completely unknown to me. Her husband was a local man called Hilton Stranaghan. She was lucky (about time she had some luck!). He was a gentle giant, one of the kindest and most pleasant people you could ever meet. They rented a lovely little flat above a detached house just outside Sudbrook, about two miles away. It did not take me long to visit them, and I could see they were very happy together. Hilton had done his national service in REME (Royal Electrical Mechanical Engineers) as a motor mechanic, and before that had worked on steam engine repairs at Severn Tunnel Junction engine sheds. He was a giant of a man, standing well over six feet, big and muscular but gently spoken and actually not confident. Being Welsh he played rugby for his regiment. He was an extraordinarily strong swimmer who could swim what seemed forever in a rough sea; he played water polo in the army and for a local team as a goalkeeper.

Staying with them on leave, my Lambretta would take me anywhere. I would travel into Newport (14 miles), Chepstow (5 miles) or, one of my favourite spots, the village of Tintern with its tourist shops, lovely restaurants and the ruins of the Cistercian Abbey. I can clearly remember my younger sister sitting on the back of my Lambretta visiting Tintern with me.

Back at camp, it was finally time for our examination. I failed, along with around one third of the others. We were given a further week to revise before resitting – the ones who had passed were given their postings and left, and I felt lonely. I sat the exam for the second time, and to my dismay everyone passed except me. The others were given their postings and disappeared the next day, leaving me on my own feeling distraught, thinking I would now be posted out as an AC1 (Aircrafts Man 1) to serve the two years left of my time as a mechanic. I had to report to the flight sergeant responsible for the examinations. We had a very long talk, him testing me verbally on my technical knowledge of what I had learnt on the course. After this he said, 'I am passing you out as a junior technician.'

Once again feeling over the moon, I was given my posting to 10 Squadron at RAF Cottesmore, Rutland. However, due to my experience over the final examination, I felt unworthy of the title 'technician' for the rest of my time in the RAF. With sadness I departed Yatesbury the following morning loaded up to the hilt with all my belongings on my trusted Lambretta, taking all my fond memories with me. As with Bridgnorth, sad to say, none of the friends I made there would ever cross my path again.

CHAPTER NINE

COTTESMORE

10 Squadron consisted of eight Handley Page Victor bombers, each designed to carry an atomic bomb. This was Britain's defence in the Cold War against a Russian attack. The technology available at the time would allow the Victors four minutes to get airborne and away to their targets inside the Soviet Union. The crews that flew in these bombers knew in their hearts there was little chance of survival: for some their targets would be deep into Russia and they had insufficient fuel to return home. Cottesmore was the jewel in the crown of Bomber Command, and we would regularly receive highly ranked politicians and heads of state of other friendly countries. I remember visits by King Hussein of Jordan, and the UK minister of defence, Duncan Sandys, who had a flight in a Victor XA937, an aircraft I had serviced.

It was a very high security camp, where everyone wore a lanyard with a photograph of themselves sealed onto a card, which gave the areas you were allowed into. I think the only area I was not allowed into was the officers' quarters.

On arriving I was escorted to Squadron Leader Sheriff, the squadron's radio officer. We had a short chat, and he called in Sergeant Davies, a Welshman who was in charge of the wireless section of the main building, which was nicknamed the 'gin palace'. He took me to a huge room, which gave me the impression of a square bashing camp, with the light glistening off the light grey highly polished floor. There were two long work-benches against the walls either side, running the whole length of the room. On these were areas set up for servicing all the pieces of equipment I had trained on. Sergeant Davies introduced me to the wireless fitters present (on the radio side the squadron only had fitters: no SACs or below). By the time he had finished showing me around, you could see who was the boss. He had a little bark on him, but I later found that he could also be very understanding.

I was also to spend a couple of days working in a hanger. I had never seen a Victor close up, and I approached the building in awe. The doors were slid right back, fully open, and there were two Victors inside, one with its nose pointing right out at me. I felt intoxicated looking at this magnificent sight in my blue RAF uniform. I felt so proud of what I had become.

After a month, I had gained sufficient experience to service the aircraft. After a brief chat with Chief Tec McKay, I was escorted into the crew room to meet other crew airmen consisting of all trades: engines, airframe, electrical, radar... Until now I had only mixed with wireless and radar men, so this was a cultural inauguration. Different trades had different values and expectations.

I was allocated XA940 as my aircraft. Chief Technician Rowe, an engine fitter, was in charge of the team. He turned out to be an extremely good person; I can't ever remember him shouting at anyone. On being introduced to the aircraft, I was instructed about all the safety precautions, the most important one being disarming the Martin Baker ejection seats, of which there were two, pilot and co-pilot, with the pin provided with each seat during maintenance. When called upon, I would service other Victors, across the other side of the airfield where 15 Squadron was based.

Most weekends, the lads would let their hair down and have a whale of a time. Oakham, around four miles away, didn't have much to offer apart from a pleasant coffee shop. Nottingham was the place for night life. It had a large dance hall, which all the best talent of the area would make a dash for. A great band played all the latest tunes. Nearer to the camp, on the same road, lay Melton Mowbray. This had a lovely coffee shop in the centre, which would be frequented by Nancy Whiskey, a folk and skiffle singer famous for her hit 'Freight Train'. I would enter, hear the juke box in the background, more often than not playing 'Freight Train', setting the mood. The local talent and RAF lads would mingle. I was very content.

Meanwhile, the squadron was making arrangements for four of the aircraft and half of the personnel to fly to RAAF (Royal Australian Air Force) Butterworth in Malaysia, for a detachment exercise lasting six weeks. I being a young technician thought I wouldn't be going; the senior technicians with most experience would do that, as maintaining the aircraft for six weeks would need the best expertise. Much to my surprise I was on the list. This made me feel really chuffed: I had never been out of the country before, let alone to the other side of the world. To prepare for this, I had to obtain a passport, all organised by the squadron (spoilt aren't I? Smashing!). We were all issued with KD (khaki dress) shirts and shorts.

The day arrived: all of us who were going (other than the air crew) would take a Bristol Britannia, a four-engine turbo prop used by the major airlines. With 1950s aircraft being limited to a maximum flying range, the journey would have to be covered in four stages. The first was to Tripoli, Libya. The RAF base was a short way in from the coast, a landing strip smack in the middle of the desert. We were billeted in large tents the size of a normal billet. The next stage was to Aden, landing at RAF Khormaksar. If I thought Libya was a dump, it was a palace compared to Aden – but luckily it was just a stop while our aircraft refuelled.

We were all looking forward to the next stop, Gan in the Maldive Islands, where we were to spend two days. The aircraft circled around the island before landing. Looking down, I could see one long runway about one mile long on a flat Island with two stretches of barren-looking brown land either side, then the sea. We had to fly in as close as possible over the end of the runway to ensure the aircraft came to a halt before dropping in to the sea at the other end.

The moment we were issued our billets – I think they were grass huts – we were all in a panic to make straight for the beach just a short walk away. It was out of a picture book: beautiful white sand stretching all around the island, which was surrounded by a coral reef. Inside the reef, the sea was flat and calm. I dropped my towel onto the beach and ran straight into the sea up to my waist (I couldn't swim at the time), despite it being rough underfoot walking on coral. After a while, I came out and lay on the sand. I felt so at home with myself; it was so silent and peaceful. Most of the other lads were chittering and chattering amongst themselves, but that didn't bother me. This was for me the sort of holiday that had only been in my dreams. Yes, the RAF looked after its own. I treated it as my home – no wonder, after my childhood.

I felt sad leaving Gan, but knowing we would have two days here again on the return home cheered me up.

Next stop was Singapore, and the RAF airbase at Changi. We were billeted here for a couple of days, which opened up an opportunity to visit the town, see the sights and visit the gift shops for souvenirs to take home. Bartering being the way to purchase items, we had some fun doing this. The Raffles Club was the sophisticated place to be seen at, but I only looked: it seemed a little posh for me. I loved the two-man trishaw or rickshaw ride; a mate of mine and I hired one to take us around at night for a tour of the city. Rickshaws carried an oil lamp on either side of the carriage at about elbow height; at the time I was wearing a short sleeved shirt; not thinking, I stuck my elbow on to the glass. My yelp of pain startled the rickshaw man, and for the next week or so I was left with a nasty scar.

Most of the rest of the time I spent gambling at cards in our billet, waiting for an aircraft to fly the squadron on its last stage to RAF Butterworth. I found I was quite proficient at cards when playing for money, pretty shrewd and calculating, especially in the bluffing games such as three-card brag and poker. Some of the lads had no idea.

Finally, an aircraft became available. I think it was a Hastings: whatever it was, the cabin was not pressurised, meaning we could not go above 10,000 ft.

Landing at Butterworth was a joy. The camp was situated in the jungle on three sides with the other next to the sea. Inside the camp, all was neat and tidy and crawling with Aussie airmen in their khaki uniforms wearing their big wide brim khaki hats. The food in their mess was superb: an enormous variety of fresh green salads, the choice of almost any meat you could think of. Our accommodation consisted of huts with sides thatched half way up and the remaining half of the side just an open space, as was the doorway. Each had six beds, with a built-in mosquito net hanging over it. I was given my own local batman, whom we were to pay 2 shillings and sixpence a week. In return, he was expected to keep my bed space clean, make the bed up, clean my brasses, and polish my shoes.

Due to the heat we started our maintenance work early in the morning, finished at midday, and had the rest of the day to ourselves. Almost every day, except the ones when I caught the ferry over to Penang, I would walk over to a lovely large swimming pool situated right by the sea. This is where I learnt to swim, having being denied this opportunity at school, due to my heart condition. Most of the squadron would finish up at the pool, and many of them would help and encourage me. I felt a right plonker: I had a fear of water, even to put my head under for a moment. One sergeant qualified in electrics proved to be a terrific help to me. He was always in the water with me, encouraging me all the time, and each day I made progress. He had me swimming a length, first where I could if necessary grab the side of the pool, then up the centre. Then I would do two lengths. Finally he had me diving in, progressing from a belly flop to a dive touching the bottom. Such help! I could never thank him enough. That's what comradeship does for you.

The squadron was preparing to send one aircraft to the American military's Clark Air Base, Philippines, for several days. Our ground crew was to go ahead for the reception of our sole Victor. Unfortunately this time I was not on the list. But it did not disappoint me; I was having a super time. The work could be hard, of course. Servicing aircraft in scorching and humid conditions proved difficult. Each aircraft was issued a portable air blower placed on the ground outside it, with a tube connecting it to the cockpit supplying fresh air. The engine fitters in particular were having serious troubles. I don't know what the particular problems were, but my guess is that the engines were overheating. Replacement parts were constantly being ordered, which had to be flown all the way from Cottesmore. As the weeks went by, a decision was made to use one Victor for spare parts, and it wasn't long before the engines went, meaning we were down to three serviceable aircraft. At the end of our detachment, there was a big push to rebuild the spare parts Victor in order to fly back home.

At the back end of the tour I caught in the pool what was named locally as Singapore ear, a common infection which created unbearable pain in the central ear channel. Every day I had to attend the camp hospital to have cotton wool forced right down the centre of each ear to release the pain – it was partially effective, relieving the pain for a short time before it slowly came back. The day came for the journey home, I had a discussion with the squadron senior flight sergeant, as they were considering whether to leave me behind to recover from my ear condition. The flight back to Singapore would be at 10,000 ft in an unpressurised aircraft, which would create pressure problems in my ears. But I was keen to get home, and to my relief it was decided to take me with them. We flew off waving goodbye to Butterworth. Our squadron flight sergeant sat by me on the flight to Changi, keeping a very close eye on me in a very caring way, which I appreciated. Looking back now, at 10,000ft with lack of oxygen my heart condition could have been a problem, but at the time I never gave it a thought. Actually, once I was in the RAF, I never considered the condition once.

I moved up from junior technician to corporal. Apart from the increase in pay, the only change was that instead of using the airmen's mess, which always involved queuing up in a long line and eating with airmen, for some of whom the level of conversation and language was not of the highest order, I would use the Corporals' Club. This was a more salubrious place, complete with its own mess and kitchen. I hardly ever had to queue. I would collect my meal from the serving counter, where there was an excellent choice of whatever I fancied, and sit down at a polished table, laid for use. The club had its own comfortable lounge with television, and a room accommodating a full-size billiard table. For work, my promotion made little or no difference, for we were a team.

Now I was more flush with cash, my thoughts turned to owning a car. I found the one I wanted (second hand, of course) in a garage on the western outskirts of Newport. It was a Jowett Javelin, a revolutionary post WW2 British car built near Bradford. The first British car to have a curved windscreen, it had a lovely streamlined silhouette, a dashboard of genuine polished walnut, real leather seats and an unusual 1486cc flat four engine. I fell for it at first sight.

I had an extended chat with the garage owner; he agreed to take Lambretta off me – I was sad to see her go; she had been my best friend for a long time – and the rest would be on hire purchase terms. As Jowett had now gone bankrupt I was concerned about service, but he promised he would service it for me. I said goodbye to my Lambretta, sat in my new car, started the engine and drove off feeling chuffed. Less clever – I only had a driving licence to drive a motorcycle or drive wagons on the airfield, and a provisional licence to drive a car. Still, at the end of my leave I drove back to camp where I could show off my new car to my friends. I now felt equal to others on the camp: some had super cars parked outside their billets and could be seen polishing them regularly with pride.

Sadly, I did not have my Javelin for long. One winter evening, when it had been snowing hard, I had a date in Nottingham which I was foolishly determined to keep. I started to drive the 30 miles there, taking it easy but still slithering all over the road. Near the end of my drive, I came up behind a very slow green Morris Minor which I decided to overtake. I gently moved out intending to allow a wide berth, and my car started skidding. It bounced into the side of the Morris and ended up hitting a thick stone wall that was part of a bridge with a railway line running underneath. Less than 10 yards away, the Morris Minor was upside down. I rushed to the aid of the person driving the Morris; as I arrived, crawling out of the rear window, a lady appeared, very shaken but uninjured – another stroke of luck.

I was fined a trivial amount for driving without due care and attention (and without L plates). My Jowett Javelin wasn't so lucky; it ended up being scrapped, and the proceeds from the insurance company went to pay off the finance company I had used to purchase the car. I finished up with nothing, other than a lesson not to be such a crazy nincompoop again.

In the last year of my service, the station had a sports day, in which everyone had to compete. We were allowed to choose our own event. It would be marked on a points system, and the squadron which got the most would be the winner.

I choose the mile. Around 25 of us lined up at the start on a marked-out grass 440 yards track. I had decided before the start to run at an even pace that I thought I could maintain the whole time. When the gun went off, there was one big mad rush almost like a sprint, which left me last by a good margin. I wasn't perturbed by this, however. I continued at my own pace, and by the end of the first lap I had already passed a number of runners. When the second lap finished I was in the middle of the field. At the start of the last lap I somehow managed to be in third position, but it was costing me. I was gasping for breath and in pain. But I started to get aspirations above myself. With encouragement from the sidelines, I could see the two runners ahead. Way ahead in first position was a tall, fit athletic-looking runner, but the lad in second place was only twenty yards from me. I put all I had left in to try and catch him – but to no avail; he kept the twenty yards to the finishing line. Still, finishing third made me feel quite pleased, and a flight sergeant originating from Rhodesia came over to me asking if I would join the station cross country team. It would involve visiting another RAF station once a week on every sports afternoon to race against them. This is how I started my running days.

Another six weeks' detachment was coming, this time to RAF Akrotiri, British Crown land located on the southern tip of Cyprus. I reckoned there was no way I'd be on the list for this – but I was. We were flying out four Victors. The maintenance crew flew out on another Britannia from RAF Lyneham.

At Akrotiri, I spent most of my time in the camp. The base covered a large area. I could do my cross country training safely, and go to the beach or the Corporals' Club, where in the evenings many of the lads would hang out and have a singalong, almost always led by Corporal Crewdson. His name fitted his use of language, which was the crudest I had ever heard – and I thought that, being in the RAF I was accustomed to foul language. He conjured the words up from who knows where, and we would all join in and have a good laugh. His version of 'Hey Ho, says Rowley' was a favourite. Looking back, Crewdson reminds me of Walker from the TV series *Dad's Army*: anything you wanted he could get. Officers found him useful.

When venturing out of camp, to visit nearby Limassol for instance, we had to stay in groups of four, as it was considered dangerous. The EOKA (a Greek Cypriot nationalist guerilla organisation) uprising was officially over, with a ceasefire in place, but many Cypriots still seemed to hold a real hate for the British. (We actually lost a man on the mission – but not to EOKA. An unfortunate wireless fitter drowned whilst snorkelling, being sick into his snorkelling mask.)

The squadron also arranged visits to interesting places. On these, we would travel in a convoy of RAF buses. On one, we visited the highest place on the island, Mount Troodos, where the top is covered in deep snow. I tried my hand at skiing but was rubbish at it. Another time, we visited Kyrenia, a port on the north coast, a pretty, relaxing place. St Hilarion Castle was included in our visit; it was a big climb to the top but well worth the effort. The views weren't stunning, but better, absolutely sensational. It was a clear day, and I could see Turkey 60 miles away. I don't think I could make the top now, except by helicopter!

Most interesting of all was my visit to Nicosia. I remember walking down Ledra Street, known to the forces at the time as Murder Mile. Until very recently it had been out of bounds to servicemen. One day, back at Akrotiri Camp, I was on my own walking on camp – I'm not sure how or why – when suddenly, coming from behind appeared a palatial shining black car. I looked up to see who was in it; looking at me, full face, smiling and giving her normal wave, was no other than the Queen, and next to her the Duke of Edinburgh, who was also waving at me. Without hesitating I waved back in a relaxed way. I know, I should have stood to attention and saluted… Recently, I looked up through Google to see if there were any records of Her Majesty's visit, but there were none. It must have been a very hush hush business.

Then our mission was over, and soon after that, so was my time in the RAF. I said goodbye to all my friends, and drove out of the camp gates on the second hand Vespa scooter I had purchased to replace the Javelin. I felt no regrets at leaving; I remained ambitious, looking forward to my life ahead. I headed for Newport, where my sister Margaret was now living in a rented flat where she had offered to put me up. I never thought of going to my father's café. I'd go anywhere but there.

CHAPTER TEN

ADJUSTING TO CIVILIAN LIFE

The RAF had been a cloistered atmosphere; everything was organised for me, mostly at the RAF's expense. Now I was out in the world. I had ambition to succeed, but was starting from scratch: I had no job waiting for me and the little savings I had would be gobbled up in no time.

The RAF did offer retraining at a government centre. There was one in Cardiff, and one of the courses they were offering was to become a television engineer. The course would be for nine months; they would put you up in digs and give you a little spending money. At the end of the course, if you passed, they would find employment for you. To get on, a test was required which I happily agreed to. It was not difficult.

The course started in two months' time, so I needed to fill them in with part-time jobs. I went to the labour exchange. A large retailer was looking for a temporary salesman selling electrical goods in its shop. They gave an interview and I started the next day – and was sacked at the end of the week. The manager wanted me to lie to customers, and I made it clear that I wasn't going to do it. Back at the exchange, there was a temporary job going for a surveying company as a 'pole man'. It was all outside work, and the easiest job I ever had. Two jovial surveyors and I marked out temporary bench marks for engineers to use when building the new M4 South Wales motorway around Newport.

I continued staying with Margaret in Newport. I joined Newport Harriers, a cross country running club.

A few days before I started the course, the training centre called me for an interview before a board of governors. I stood in front of the table they were sitting at, and was informed that I could start 'on trial'. I felt gobsmacked. I told them that I had been promised a place on a course. Nothing had been said about a trial. They carried on looking self-assured and pompous, and one of them said that my marks hadn't been good enough. I replied that my marks had been about 95%. He made no reply, and I said coolly that I would not go on the course. I was furious inside, but would not bow down to this lot. I was about to walk away when the head of the college, who had not said anything until now, interrupted and said they would take me without any strings attached.

Looking back now I could have harmed my future. Pride comes before a fall.

The college paid for my digs in Cardiff, and I went on to successfully complete the course, and the college kept their word, finding me a job at Merthyr Tydfil working for Rediffusion.

During my time at college, I would often make visits to my mother, who had now moved to the Langland Bay Golf Club, with her husband serving as steward of the club. When it was time to go to Merthyr, I had no money for digs: I asked her if she would lend me some to pay for my first week, and I would pay her back over the next several weeks. She willingly loaned me the cash. After everything that had happened in the past, I still felt a bond with her.

Arriving in Merthyr, I received a warm welcome from the service manager and service staff. The branch manager, Mr Hayes, came up from the shop to introduce himself to me. He was an ex-army officer; I could see who was the boss. The service manager had arranged digs for me with the Berry family a few roads away. They were welcoming, good people. Mrs Berry showed me upstairs to the bedroom I would be using. The house was clean and tidy, with a homely feel about it. At work, I was repairing televisions that the outside engineers brought in for repair. I enjoyed the work – but was on the lowest pay grade.

The service manager and I both reckoned I was one of the best engineers they had, so I asked Mr Hayes for a rise up to the next pay grade. He told me he would look into it and have a word with the service manager. I thanked him and left it at that, but started making a list of the repairs I was completing. A week went by and I heard nothing, then Mr Hayes made one of his regular visits to us. It gave me the opportunity to ask him about my request for a pay rise. He gave me a load of waffle about how it depended on how much work I was doing. I then produced the list of work that I had completed that week. I got my rise – but what a fuss to get it. Little did he know that the service manager and I had colluded together.

My sister Margaret and Hilton moved to Swansea to live nearer my mother. Hilton had a canoe, and would take it to Langland Bay. It was summer now, and Hilton and I would go out into the bay canoeing (I would wear a life-jacket; he didn't require one due to his swimming prowess). One Saturday, we decided to venture out into the bay. The sea was fierce with huge rolling waves and we had immense difficulty trying to launch the canoe against them. Once launched, every time a wave hit us we were thrown out of the boat. While my feet could touch the bottom I didn't mind, but once we were out of my depth and thrown out, that was enough for me. I told Hilton, and we called it a day. The following afternoon we were down the beach again for another try. Now the sea was very calm. We spoke to a man there who owned a beach hut and turned out to be a local doctor. He said to us, 'You should have been here yesterday – there were two nutters trying to launch a canoe!' We replied that the nutters were us, and we all had a giggle.

Back at work, I requested a transfer to the Rediffusion branch in Newport. There was no position for a TV Engineer, but they offered me one as linesman engineer. This entailed maintaining the repeater amplifiers that covered the Newport region, going out into the field servicing amplifiers, and if necessary replacing them and bringing the faulty ones back to the workshops where I would repair them. (I now had a driving license, courtesy of Rediffusion Merthyr, who had paid for the driving lessons. Thank you, Merthyr.)

I accepted the position, found digs in Rothesay Road, Newport, a convenient place not far from the track where the Harriers headquarters were, and not far from the centre of town, where night life would take place. While still short of money, I was receiving more now and had a few bob to spare so decided to buy a car. One of the Harriers, Tom Wood, had a cousin living near the track who sold second-hand cars. Tom came with me to have a look at a car he was selling, an Austin A105, a big-engined, roomy car in a light cream colour in super condition. I looked at it, liked it, and bought it.

At my new job, I had to report to the overall service manager, responsible for the still expanding wiring system of the Newport region. He introduced me to Roy, a pleasant, friendly chap who I would report directly to and who took me around the region showing me the ropes. I was given a van which I had to return every night. All the wiremen of the region would meet up every morning at a local café which had a super juke box, playing all the latest pop tunes (Frank Ifield was popular at the time). I'd join them, to find out what they were doing and what problems they were having. I liaised with their foreman, another pleasant smiling person and made myself popular with all.

The Ringland Estate had just been completed. Rediffusion were wiring it for the reception of piped TV, with green BT-style boxes around the place. The wiremen had fed the cables into the boxes; I had to install a repeater amplifier and set it up working. The big boss Mr Hancock came to inspect the first one I did. I had labelled everything up making it easy to identify everything, which had never been done before. He gave me glowing compliments on my accomplishment; it made me feel chuffed.

Roy was a good pal to me; he would allow me to sneak off early in the afternoon to get to the track for training the other side of town. I enjoyed training. It became a social event with Harrier friends. Quite a few had run for Wales, not only cross country but also track, and there were Harriers that had competed for Great Britain. I became friendly with Howard Davies, who would run the 400 metres in the 1968 Mexico Olympics: we would often walk home together. Another very good friend of mine was Mike Rowland, who represented Wales in the marathon at the 1970 and 1978 Commonwealth Games. And there was the Newport legend Tom Wood, who ran the 1958 Commonwealth Games marathon for Wales. I was always a tail end charley, bringing up the rear, but I enjoyed the sport. A runner once said to me, 'It's like bashing your head against a brick wall; it's fantastic when you stop.'

Back at work, the TV service manager offered me overtime, working on outside TV repair calls. I jumped at the chance of time and a half. However, I was becoming restless and wanted to progress with my career. Rentaset was a national company with a reputation for employing the best TV engineers. They had a branch in Newport, and I decided to apply to them. I gave my CV to Mr Baker, the local manager, who put me forward for an interview. It was a stiff test. After an interview with the head recruiter who had travelled from Swindon head office, came a hundred tick box questions. I then had to find three separate faults deliberately placed on a TV, with him looking over my shoulder and me explaining exactly what I was doing and why. I thought I was back in the RAF. At the end, he offered me a job.

When I handed my notice in at Rediffusion, the Branch Manager, Mr Alwen, who had never even bothered with me, called me via the TV service manager for a meeting in his office. He used all the persuasive qualities he had to prevent me from leaving. I was polite to him but my answer was 'no'. As I left the room he said, 'You'll be sorry'. I thought, 'you don't look so superior now. You're grovelling.' I had information before the meeting that the chief engineering manager of the region had asked him to prevent me from leaving.

The engineers at Newport Rentaset, about 15 of them, were all on a different level to most of the TV engineers I had worked with. They were self confident, quiet, not pushy, respectful of others. They could hold an intelligent conversation. It was said this branch could run itself, though looking back now, I disagree. Mr Baker was softly spoken and had control of everything. Any problems, he would nip them in the bud. He had served as an army sergeant paratrooper dropped in at Arnhem, so nothing fazed him. I was proud to be working with the best.

Meanwhile, I was spending as much time as I could running. Newport Harriers were an integrated bunch. We would exchange ideas on training methods and learn from each other. Already, some of the very top runners nationally had their own coaches. I couldn't see the point of this. I had a misconceived idea at the time that if you wanted to achieve something, all you had to do was just work extra hard for it, meaning in this case train harder and longer, and you would make it happen. No advice or guidance needed.

My running wasn't all rubbish. I actually won a race at Newport County football ground, Somerton Park. Around the pitch was a sandy track used for greyhound racing. The track being roughly 440 yards, Harriers' administrators, in conjunction with greyhound people, had arranged a four-lap race as a promotion for the club, along with some interest for the spectators during a break in the dog races.

There were eight thousand people present. About twenty Harriers lined up at the start. There were some good milers who I knew could tank me, but I had a plan. I would stay at the back, then stick to the field as long as I could. The gun went off; we were away with a rush to the first bend to get in pole position. I let the rush go, tracking the field at the rear and keeping as close as possible to the inside of the track. After the first lap we were all strung out in a more or less straight line with no gaps, so this put me around 25 yards behind the leader. I was feeling OK and running smoothly within myself. Runners just in front of me were now starting to allow gaps to appear, so I moved around them to close the gaps up. Half way round I had passed three runners, and by the end of the lap a few more. The crowd were beginning to chant and cheer which helped in giving a little motivation. I knew I would not disgrace myself in this race and not come last.

At the end of lap three, I was still passing runners. I had no idea who was in the lead. The crowd was going berserk with encouragement. I was expecting a real burn up on the last lap. I gritted my teeth, keeping all my focus and concentration directly in front of me. I was still with them as we entered the start of the last bend. I was still keeping tight to the inside of the track. I could hear the crowd cheering, as if they were in a misty fog coming from a distance. Coming off the last bend I was in third position – and Roger Bannister flashed into my mind. I was aching all over, gasping for breath. I could see the finish line and made one last desperate challenge to get in front of the leader, Glyn Sullway. I drew next to his shoulder. We were now running neck and neck; the more I tried, the more he tried. We arrived at the finish together and I made one final lunge across the line – I had won! As Winston Churchill would say, this was my finest hour. It was the pinnacle of my running; it would get no better for me.

I was happy in my digs at this time. Mr and Mrs Young were a lovely old couple, now retired. Mrs Young was so caring; she just couldn't do enough for me. I had my own bedroom, with breakfast in the mornings; she allocated me my own room downstairs for me to relax in when I came in after work during wintertime. An open hearth fire in the room would be stacked with coal and burning full ahead. She would bring me in a beautifully cooked dinner. Yes, you could say I was spoilt.

Then completely out of the blue, she asked me to leave. I asked her what I had done to offend her, and she said 'nothing'. She was getting a young lady to take my place who would help her around the house with chores. I felt a little embarrassed. I had to find some new digs pretty sharp, as the young lady would be coming at the weekend, and asked around the track area if anyone was looking to take a lodger in.

I found someone that was. I will call her Mrs Doubtfire, as she looked rather like the character played by Robin Williams in the movie decades later. I knocked on her front door, she answered it, I enquired if she took lodgers in and she said she did. I followed her upstairs, where she showed me the bedroom I would have, somewhat small, but I thought 'that will do'. Back downstairs, she explained I would have breakfast with her family, no husband but four young grown-up children. She would supply me a meal in the evening, which I would eat in the kitchen. I can't say I was happy about the place, but being desperate I accepted.

I didn't like the lodgings and liked Mrs Doubtfire even less. It was the summer, so I spent most of my time at the track, keeping away from the house as much as possible; after training I would regularly go with several of the lads for a small glass of cider at a local pub. I wasn't there long before I had a disagreement with her and decided to leave. I knew how she would react, so waited until first thing Monday morning, then quietly packed all my belongings in my car. I went back into the kitchen where she was, with exactly one week's lodge money clenched in my hand, put it down on her kitchen table and announced I was now leaving the digs. Without waiting for an answer I made a rapid beeline for my car, shut and locked the door. She was after me like a bullet; as I was starting the car, she grabbed the door handle whilst shouting and banging on my window. I drove away. I had nowhere to go, though I was not bothered too much about that as I could sleep in the car. The incident upset me, however.

By the time I reached work, she had telephoned Mr Baker, trying to have me sacked with a pack of untruths. He called me into his office and explained what she had said. I gave him my side of the story. He was all very quietly spoken about it; he knew the type of person I was and took sympathy with me. At that moment I broke down, tears running down my face. I went back upstairs to carry on my work; he must have mentioned it to Ernie for there was a lot of sympathy floating round for me. The next thing I knew, in came Ron the storeman offering me digs with him, which I happily accepted without even seeing his house.

I represented Newport Harriers in the British Cross Country Championships at Blackpool and at Parliament Hill Fields. The race was 9 miles long, much of it through mud, not the shorter version as it is today. I normally finished just over half way down the field but Oh, how I enjoyed it! I remember seeing Gerry North and Bruce Tulloh, two icons of the time battling it out toe to toe at Blackpool – a contest I saw at close quarters as I was being lapped by them. Tulloh was running, as he always did, in bare feet, which should have given him the advantage on that muddy course, but on that day, Gerry North pipped him.

Another high point of my running days was competing in the Welsh Marathon Championships at Port Talbot. I did some preparation for it, covering around twenty miles on Wednesday evenings for four weeks before the event, then 'training down' (relaxing the training regime) several days before the competition. The race would be three laps, starting along the Aberavon front then circling round the area. It included three steep hill climbs – not exactly built for fast times. There were around 35 runners, not only from Wales but all over. You may ask why only 35 runners when nowadays a thousand would not be considered unusual. But we were not joggers but runners, all capable of covering 10 miles in under the hour.

We lined up across the road, paused, then we were away. I tucked in at the rear, intending to run my usual even pace to allow me to obtain a respectable time. I not being alone in thinking this, a small bunch quickly developed around me. The rest were quickly well strung out in front of us. I was running at little more than jogging speed, just the pace I wanted. We continued as a group through ten miles; I was feeling quite relaxed and our time was OK. However, from here on things started to happen. The group started to split up, one by one slowly dropping. I found myself running alone, going further away from those I had been running with, but with no one in sight in front of me.

I kept going at my own speed and rhythm. At the end of the second lap along Aberavon beach front, around eighteen miles, I saw a bunch of around six runners. I rapidly closed on them then ran past like a puff of wind, as if they were standing still. I knew them all by name, as they did me; as I passed them we looked across at each other, giving each other encouragement. Looking up the road I could now see a runner in the distance, but it was harder work to catch him, especially as we had arrived at the bottom of the steep hill. I worked harder than I should have going up it and passed him just before the top.

My legs began to feel like lead weights. I forgot about any other runner, and just focused on finishing. With about two miles to go, I stopped running and started to walk, but still with a sense of urgency. As I walked into the last feeding station, at 25 miles, the time-keepers said if I kept going I could do under three hours. I gulped down my drink of water, and changed up several gears. I had one and a quarter miles to go, and had no one in sight for me to aim for: I just ran as fast as I could. I entered the home straight on Aberavon sea front. The finish line was about 400 yards away. I was really knackered now but gave it my all. I crossed the line – in 2 hours 58 minutes – and lay on the floor to recover. I was so chuffed; I had broken 3 hours, considered a good run in those days. The icing on the cake for me was that looking at the times from the 25-mile mark to the finish I was the fourth fastest. The field had included many internationals, including Juan Taylor, who won with a time of 2 hours 15 minutes and the legendary Bill Adcock, running in his first marathon, who came second with 2 hours 19 minutes.

However, at this time my training was mainly focused on the mile. It was considered the blue riband of the track. All youngsters like me could remember BBC commentator David Colman commentating at the White City on runners like Bannister, Ibbotson, Tulloh, Chataway, Kuts, Zatopek, Pirie... At first, I would struggle to go under five minutes on the track, but training with the Harriers my times slowly improved. One evening we competed in an interclub meeting against the Cardiff clubs. Electing to run in the mile I ran my best time of 4 minutes 42 seconds. Two weeks later I repeated the same time. This gave me a spur for next year to aim for 4 minutes 30 econds, at the time to be considered county standard.

I entered for the mile in the Welsh Championships taking place at the usual place, Maindy Stadium, Cardiff. There were two heats, with six to qualify from each heat. I ran in the first one. I had decided to stay around sixth position, track the leaders for two laps, then see what happened. When we set off the pace was slow – but there was a quality field. I moved to fifth position during the third lap to try to cover myself for the last one, which I expected to be a burn up. It was. But I kept my position. I waited until coming off the last bend, then moved across to kick past the runners in front of me. I caught the leader, Bill Stitfole. Everyone was shouting for me, as the underdog, to win, but I thought no, all I need is to qualify, so I kept half a yard behind him.

The final was less dramatic: I finished half way down. However, as a result of qualifying for it, I received a letter of invitation to compete in the mile at the prestigious Welsh Games. It was at Maindy Stadium again, but this time eight thousand athletics followers were there. A good few in the stadium knew me, and I was hoping not to embarrass myself, as I was up against some that had broken 4.00 minutes for the mile. They were from all over the world: Australia, New Zealand, and several high altitude Kenyan runners. I warmed up alongside these from about an hour before the race, an experience in itself. It was a beautiful sunny afternoon, with the crowd in light short-sleeve shirts. We were called up for the start, about 15 to 20 of us. I had decided to take my place at the rear, then hang on until I had nothing left. The first lap was very pacy, the leader going through in around 60 seconds. I was still with most of the field, going through in 65. By the second lap, I was still only just hanging on. I managed to do the half mile in 2 minutes 10 seconds, but my tank was now empty. I told myself that whatever I did now was a bonus. After the first bend, I was gasping for air with my legs feeling as heavy as sledge hammers. The rest of the field pulled away – but I was not done yet. I thought 'I haven't come here to step off the track, as some would.'. My pride wouldn't let me. I struggled the last laps. Apart from exhaustion, I felt embarrassed; I could feel pity from the crowd. Maybe the performance was embarrassing, but would I do it again? Someone with my medical background would be over the moon to run against the best; as it turned out that was my only chance.

Before we move on from my Newport Harrier days, I must mention the day I ran against Basil Heatley, a Coventry Godiva Harrier who was at the time the world ten-mile record holder. The race was from Hereford to Ross on Wye, 14 miles. There were no bypasses or motorways in those days; running in the Ross on Wye road race meant running on the main road, keeping to the left hand side. I'm not sure how many started, probably 40 or 50. We stood on the line; the gun went off – and that was the last I saw of Basil Heatley, as he disappeared into the distance. I just enjoyed running a steady race on a lovely Saturday afternoon, except right at the end, where I turned left up the hill over the river Wye and let rip all the way, around a mile, to the finish. I finished half way down the field.

CHAPTER ELEVEN

MEETING THE BEST PERSON IN THE WORLD

That summer I stayed on holiday at my sister Margaret's flat near the centre of Swansea. I did a bit of training, but one evening I decided to venture out to Mumbles and go dancing at the Tivoli Ballroom, where the young local talent would gather. I entered the place on my own; everyone seemed to know each other, chattering and chittering away. I felt isolated. In fact, I was just about to meet the best person in the world, who would turn out to be my wife, lover, best friend and a person I could trust, something I hadn't truly done since my mother broke the promise she made to me about coming to live with her (I'd been 15 at the time). This person would turn my life completely around, and we would go on to have two fantastic children.

This young lady caught my eye, wearing a gorgeous pink flowery dress, looking demure and beautiful. She was chatting to another woman. I casually walked over and requested a dance with her. She said 'yes'. I asked her name, and she said 'Pat'. We danced. We didn't say a lot, but feeling her body against mine, I desired her. I escorted her back to her friend, whom she introduced as Sylvia – and who I quickly discovered chatted more than most. Pat appeared to be a quiet person, but Sylvia made up for this in abundance. It was soon clear that Sylvia was trying her best to have us both dated up. I was happy with that, as I always felt uncomfortable around pretty girls; I would always lose my tongue.

Silvia had her way. Pat and I met up again before I headed back to Newport, and she agreed that I would travel down next weekend after work to see her. I couldn't wait for the weekend to come… When it arrived, I was off like a shot to Swansea.

This became a regular event. I would stay with Margaret. Pat and I would spend much of our time together travelling around the district. She showed me places I had not been to. I drove her to her home to meet her parents; it turned out to be a farm on the edge of the town at the little village of Glais. I remember parking outside the farmhouse, getting out of the car, then going around to open the door for her to get out. Her mum and dad (plus Bob the farm sheep dog, wagging his tail) came out to greet me, with a warm welcome on their faces. They introduced themselves: Elise and Jack (known locally as Jack the Garth, after the name of his farm). We went inside. Pat had a younger brother, John, a shy young lad of eight. Both her parents originated from the nearby village of Skewen. Her mum also spoke Welsh, and looked a typical Welsh lady, short and stocky, with a shyness about her. Her dad was a tall, upright, proud man with thinning ginger hair, also quite shy. He wore a flat cap.

I became part of the family. In the evenings when I would take Pat back home, we would all sit around their kitchen table having supper. It was very much 'you take us as you find us'; nothing posh or fancy – exactly how I enjoyed it. Here mum would always make an appetising supper from bits and pieces. If it was late, her parents would go to bed and Pat and I would chat around a lovely open coal fire, before I returned to my sister's.

Pat's father had wanted her to do well at school, and so she had done, starting at the small village school at Glais. Amongst her class she was the only one to pass the eleven plus, then go on to Llwyn-y-bryn Grammar School for Girls, Swansea. It was a long trip there and back; early in the morning she would walk from the farm to Clydach, where she would catch a public bus into Swansea city centre, change to catch another. Pat's father, who I know she was very close to and to whom she would look for guidance in all things, had aspirations for her to become a doctor. Pat had completed her first year in the sixth form when an opportunity arose for her to get a job in Morriston Hospital, around two miles from her farm, to train as a radiographer. She accepted the opportunity and left school. When we first met she was around nineteen.

I applied for a transfer from Rentaset Newport to Rentaset Swansea. The company quickly agreed, and in next to no time I became a Swansea engineer. I felt a cultural change. People had started work there after the boom in TV rental. As long as you could change a valve and install a set, that was good enough. They were paid at the lowest grade C, and far too many of them were at this standard. A communist-style shop steward didn't help. However, the top engineers were up to Newport standards, which was something.

Pat and I got engaged, planning to marry in a year's time. We both started saving to buy a house. I would work all the overtime I could – there was plenty. Pat, who had now qualified, was doing all the 'on call' that she could. I wondered at times why a charming, beautiful girl full of intelligence, with a grammar school education, would want to marry a boy like me, from the bad side of a council estate who had been an illiterate dunce at school.

During our days off we would do much of our courting along Gower's coast. There are many beaches, with countless sand dunes hidden among the marram grass: a paradise for courting couples, hidden from the world. These were great times.

One time was not so great. I telephoned Pat one lunchtime while I was making service calls in Morriston, and completely out of the blue she said she didn't want to see me again. I said, 'Why? What have I done to offend you?' She said nothing. I felt so distraught and pleaded with her to see me again. I remember standing in the telephone box with tears running from my eyes. She eventually agreed to see me. We met up again but never really discussed the incident. It was forgotten, and we happily continued on as before.

We went house hunting together. A good new semi-detached house around Swansea in these bygone days would cost around £2,500. There were some dream homes in Swansea West, but we resisted them, keeping to our budget. Finally, we found a place we both liked. It was in the village of Ynystawe, on the hillside overlooking her father's farm with the picturesque River Towey flowing below. There were around twenty steps up to the front door, and the views from the front windows were ecstatic: a beautiful green valley with low hills on the horizon, fields everywhere like a patchwork quilt, dotted with trees. We were both excited, and went back to discuss the house with Pat's wise father. He knew the builder, a local firm that don't normally build houses.

As the house was unpainted inside, we were offered £100 off, with the builder offering to sell us any paint or hardware goods we needed at trade prices. We had a final viewing and decided to go for it.

Pat worked tirelessly like a Trojan. I did, too. Those school woodwork lessons from Mr Walker suddenly proved useful. We emulsioned all the walls with light, airy colours, painted all the woodwork white, and felt proud of our achievement. We gathered chattels. When we bought new, we bought quality items: a Younger's set of elegant solid teak wardrobes and a good quality bed. All the rest came second hand from Pat's mum: an old fashioned solid wooden table, a couple of chairs, a large rug to go in our lounge, not forgetting a broken down Baby Belling cooker which I managed to revive.

Our wedding day was drawing nearer. I wanted both my parents to attend. After their divorce they had never met or wanted to. My family said that I could have one to come but would never get both. I had other ideas. I knew my mother would come, but was not sure of my father, whom I had not seen since leaving the RAF. I was planning to take Pat down to Exeter to meet him, when suddenly one day I received a telephone call from my stepmother. She was distraught. My stepbrother Stephen, who was only seventeen, had suddenly become dangerously ill with meningitis. She wanted me to come down to Devon and help them in any way I could. Without hesitation I said I would. I collected Pat from work; we had a bite to eat at the farm, then left that evening. Looking back now it probably wasn't wise to take her. In those days there were no motorways, Severn bridge crossings or town bypasses; we had to drive to Gloucester to cross the Severn, and the route took us on twisty winding roads, through every little village or city, taking probably three times longer than it would today. We arrived at my father's café late in the evening and they were all in tears. I was too late. Stephen had passed away.

In his bedroom, where he had lain crying with excruciating pain trying to hang on to life, there were splatters of blood all over the wall. It turned out that the doctor had refused to come out to see him. My father had him before a G.M.C. committee which he attended at their head office London, but the doctor was not struck off. They closed ranks.

Pat and I had arranged to be back at work Monday morning. I said I would to return for Stephen's funeral; we said our sad goodbyes then departed late afternoon for home. Several days later Pat and I decided it would be best if I travelled down to my father's on my own, arranging to arrive the night before.

There were many folk arriving at the house from early morning as the cortége would leave from here and drive up a narrow lane to the small village of Sowton less than a mile away, where the burial would take place in the picturesque church grounds. My father was in almost uncontrollable distress. After the funeral, the family and all the mourners returned to his bungalow where food was being served. I stayed that night, then over breakfast told them I would visit them again, said a sad goodbye and made my way back home.

I waited a respectable time before asking my father to attend our wedding. I explained that I wanted both my parents to be present. After some discussion he agreed, as long as Jack Hughes wasn't there. That was easy, as there wasn't a chance in hell I was going to allow that anyway. I still had to make some concessions. Pat and I agreed that my stepsisters Rosemary would be a bridesmaid with Heather as a guest: I didn't have any problem with that. I had to agree for my stepmother to come otherwise my father would not have done. I got what I wanted.

The day of our wedding arrived; I slept in our new house the night before. A wedding car took me and my best man, Hilton, to the Seion Welsh Chapel, Glais, Pat's family chapel. Hilton and I entered the chapel in our morning suits. I glanced either side as I walked, acknowledging those in attendance. Everyone I wanted was present.

We then began to wait. Some might have begun to think that Pat had had cold feet and changed her mind, but not me. I felt cool; I knew she would turn up. She eventually arrived looking gorgeous in her wedding dress. She walked down the aisle and stood next to me. We looked, smiling, at each other. She seemed a little nervous. It transpired that she was late because the driver of the wedding car, after dropping me off had forgotten the small matter of collecting the bride. Only after Pat's dad had telephoned to enquire what was happening did the driver realise. What a plonker!

We gave our wedding vows. Years float by like fast moving clouds – there were good times with dark; sun one minute, clouds the next; it's part of life. Through all the ups as well as the downs, we have both kept our wedding vows. They are stronger now than ever. Following those vows, Tudor, the Welsh-speaking vicar, led us into a side room. The register was completed, and we made our way for a wedding breakfast at The Osborne Hotel, Langland Bay. It was a fashionable place to dine in those days, all the *crachach* (Welsh for posh), would eat there. Our dining room had a window running full length, with a gorgeous view directly over plummeting rocks and out to the horizon. Pat in her wedding gown eclipsed such natural beauty. We sat down together – she seemed much more relaxed now – and chatted with her bridesmaids, cousins Mire and Rosemary in their beautiful turquoise dresses.

After the wedding breakfast came the speeches. I had not been looking forward to this, and neither had Hilton. But I had mine written down. It was very short and got straight to the point. Even when I was a boy, if ever I had to stand up to speak, even in front of four or five people, I would freeze with my mind going blank. It wasn't until my late fifties I began to overcome this phobia. But all went well that day.

We made our goodbyes to the guests, and Pat and I were taken to Swansea Station where her family waved us off for our first journey as a married couple, to London. Arriving at Paddington station we intended taking a taxi, when a car pulled up in front of us and the driver asked if we were looking for a taxi. I said we were; he said he was a private hire firm; he showed me his credentials then asked where we were going. I answered, Regent Palace Hotel, and he said 'hop in'. When arrived at our destination, he placed our luggage onto the pavement and I asked how much I owed him. He said, '£15, sir.'

I looked in his face with startled amusement and said, 'How much?' He must have twigged that I wasn't born yesterday; he came back with, 'What's wrong with £5, sir?' I felt embarrassment, apologised to him for my misunderstanding of the situation, then gave him a whacking great tip, trying to make amends. But Pat confirmed with me afterwards that I had heard correctly and he had first asked for £15. We live and learn!

We had arrived late at night, but were in no mood to miss the night life going on around Piccadilly Circus, the heart of London. The statue at the centre, Eros, a boy with a bow and arrow, the Greek symbol of selfish love for its own desires. We walked round watching the hustle and bustle. People were laughing and cheering. Neon lights flashed and flickered colours of the rainbow. Touts were touting. Night ladies stood on corners. There were strange side doors, where we feared to tread, with a muscle man outside talking and gawking plus eying the rest. We bought a burger, the best we had ever had, then, completely relaxe, retired to bed. Did we sleep? Well you'll have to guess; I'll say no more except that was the best part of the whole experience.

We arose early for breakfast, not wanting to miss the sights, spent all day looking around, then back to the Regent Palace, where we relaxed for the rest of the night. Keeping to our budget, we had arranged to stay two nights. Pat's Aunty Betty had kindly offered to put us up at her flat in Harrow for several more – then it was home to Wales. We arrived proudly at our brand new house. I clearly remember stepping forward with my key, opening the door, picking Pat up and carrying her in.

Back at work, we grabbed every opportunity for extra work to build our home up. We started on the floor boards, then bought plain woollen carpets – only the best; it gave such a feeling of warmth.

My running had gone AWOL, but I started up again. The views from our windows were so inviting to train. I would normally take a six-mile circuit around leafy lanes in sight of the house, where Pat could glimpse me from time to time. I would race road or cross country on Saturdays, as I had moved reluctantly to Swansea Harriers. In some ways that was good; they were low in numbers, meaning I could make the first team. But I did miss Newport Harriers and my mates.

I remember one New Year's Eve, travelling from Swansea to Merthyr Tydfil for the annual Nos Galan road race, which is timed to end when the clock strikes midnight. On this particular year Merthyr lay under five inches of snow, and with snow continuing to fall and runners arriving in large numbers, we weren't sure if Bernard Baldwin, our organiser, would call the race off. We all wanted to run, so we did. While changing for the race I met the legendary distance runner Gordon Pirie, breaker of six world records. He had written a book, *Running Wild,* about himself; I possessed a copy which I conveniently brought with me. We had a chat and he signed my book and dated it, 1st Jan 64. I treasured that book then. I still treasure it now.

There were around 600 of us. It was tough running through snow, despite wearing cross country studs. I recall one particular hill with terraced houses on either side, how each local encouraged us and how their houses lit up the night. It was an event to remember.

It did have a downside: Pat was not with me. She did not become a keen follower of athletics, and this was a contentious matter between us, particularly when I went away for the day running. I wanted my freedom – not to drink and womanise, but just to run.

Once our home was looking good, we decided to splash out on a 14-foot Lynton touring caravan. They were fashionable in those days. We being young, with adventure in our blood, planned to take a fortnight's holiday touring Europe. I can clearly recall leaving the farm with the blue Riley saloon car I had recently bought hitched up to the caravan and fully loaded up with provisions for two weeks. We drove to Dover through London, past Buckingham Palace, arrived at the port then drove onto the ferry to Zeebrugge. We passed through Germany on its awesome Autobahns. Having a caravan enabled us to stop to eat or sleep whenever we felt like it. I remember we stopped at a typical Autobahn lay-by – large compared to our standard British offerings. Driving into a small wooded area, we parked up, entered the caravan, drew the curtains as it was daytime, then went to bed. The next thing, we were awoken by a man's voice outside, shouting 'Halten Verboten!' a number of times. I said to Pat, 'Let's be quiet and pretend we're not here, he might go away.' It worked.

Arriving at our destination, Austria, we made a two-day stop in the Tyrol where we unhitched the van, leaving us the freedom to drive around. This area, the Ötztal Valley, became one of our favourites. We drove on to stay for two days at a village campsite just outside Salzburg, visiting the beautiful historic city: more memories to treasure. Next stop was to be Vienna. We chose the Autobahn route. Pat was driving, when completely out of the blue our caravan started snaking. Pat started to wrestle with the steering wheel, turning it one way then the other. Out of the corner of my left eye, I could see the caravan at about a 45 degree angle to us. She was now in a panic state, shouting at me what to do. With my right hand I grabbed the left hand side of the steering wheel, then gently coaxed us out of this horrendous snaking. As we came out of the snake, huge lorries came roaring past us; had it been a second earlier, there would have been one almighty pile up.

We made for a campsite I had earmarked, 20 km outside the city at Laxenburg. It had marvellous facilities, including a typical Austrian restaurant. On our last evening there we choose to dine in it. It was a romantic night to remember, a beautiful Austrian meal accompanied with a violinist standing directly facing us at our candlelit table playing typical Austrian music.

Next morning we made our way to Graz, southern Austria, a beautiful city famous for its clock tower, then moved on over snowbound tips of the Alps via the Brenner Pass into Italy, making for Bolzano. As we were nearing Bolzano we came across a farm offering a campsite in a beautiful orchard full of apple trees laden with fruit. The site was basic but heavenly. Bolzano was an interesting place, especially its market with very cheap wine.

While travelling up a twisting road high in the Tyrolean Dolomites, our car started to overheat, accompanied by a smell. I pulled in to find out what was wrong, lifted up the bonnet and started to turn the radiator cap, when completely without warning boiling water shot high up almost hitting me in the face. I waited for the radiator and engine to cool down, before moving off again, but the car did not feel right.

Our holiday time was now running out, and we started to make our way back to Zeebrugge. However, as we progressed our Riley was becoming sicker. We limped into Zeebrugge for our ferry crossing. By this time the car had difficulty starting. Arriving at Dover, we were assisted off the ferry, but we were now stuck. I contacted the AA; they sent someone to look at the car and he said that the engine was clapped out due to the overheating. It was a Sunday, too...

The AA man arranged for us to be taken to a local car park, where a specialist garage could repair the engine. It would require stripping down, new piston rings and bearings. We slept in the van, and the garage completed the job the next day, in time for us to depart late afternoon. The repair cost made me choke, but we had had a fantastic adventure, one never to forget. We both returned to work refreshed.

A problem was brewing up for me with our shop steward, who for the sake of the book I shall call Mr Kommie. He appeared to have most people in his pocket, except the manager Mr R. The inevitable time came when I had a confrontation with him. There was an incident with one of our aerial riggers, and Mr Kommie used his usual manoeuvres, going around poisoning people's minds, with his little meetings in the firm's time at their local tea haunt. He called a union meeting the following day at our workshop. The meeting was well attended, with all our engineers and aerial riggers (each with a young lad): in total around 30 people. I noted that the riggers with their assistants outnumbered the engineers. Kommie called the meeting to order, did 90% of the talking, then called for a vote. At that point I interrupted, asking if he was having these young boys to vote on whether engineers, with families to support, should go out on strike. There was then a lot of chattering of discontentment amongst the engineers, and under pressure, Mr Kommie agreed that the lads could not vote. A count was made; common sense won the day and there was no strike. Kommie tried to look calm, but I could see inside he was fuming.

I now had a dangerous enemy. The meeting dispersed with the workshop engineers staying behind. I remember Stan, a super engineer, commenting, 'Well Malc, that's the first time Kommie ever lost.' It gave me a sense of justice and pride.

As I walked along the corridor to leave, Mr R was coming toward me. As I passed him I could see how the look on his face had changed from tense and taut to a smile. I commented, 'You can put that one down to me.'

A short while later, for some reason which I don't recall, Mr Kommie decided that I would be sent to Coventry. Nobody was supposed to speak to me. It had no effect on me at all, and in any case almost all the engineers ignored his directive. They had more intelligence than he gave them credit for.

A while after, he left the company and someone else became shop steward. He wasn't very good, and I was approached to take over from him. I did not want to do so, but in the end I reluctantly agreed. As shop steward I felt I had a responsibility to attend local union meetings. This was an eye opener for me. You would have five or six attending, nearly always the same people, voting amongst themselves on actions that others would have to carry out. It could even be to strike or not to – all under the name of democracy. I was gobsmacked.

On one occasion, there was a dispute about a new pay agreement on a national basis. Our national union officer Roy Sanderson called a union meeting in Cardiff. I and around 200 plus engineers attended in a large room with Mr Sanderson plus his entourage on stage. He addressed the meeting explaining why the strike had been called but it was for us to decide. I felt his speech was not a balanced presentation; he was pushing to have the strike. He asked for any questions. I raised my hand; he asked me to speak; I stood up addressed him straight off the top of my head. I tried to be as constructive and polite as I could – no effing or blinding – but I did attack him on the grounds that in my opinion he was responsible for engineering this proposed strike. I did end up pointing at him, saying, 'Yes, you, Mr Sanderson'. There was then complete silence in the room. I sat down to cool myself off. I knew I had come on a bit too strong. Later I stood up to apologise to him for the manner in which I spoke. He scoffed at me saying he'd 'met my sort', but in such a way that I could see I had got to him. A strike was called initially for one day. Although not approving of it, on the morning of the strike I went in to ensure there were no engineers working. There weren't. My job finished, I went home. It was the only strike day as the dispute was then settled. I learnt a great deal from my shop steward days.

Around that time, Pat and I had arranged a week's summer holiday with our caravan touring North Wales. Our first night we stayed at Brontlyst, a lovely restful site. From there we moved on to a site next to Bala Lake. We drove out of the site, turning right onto the main road. The turning is on a bend – and suddenly a motorcycle came haring round that bend, on our side of the road and going too fast. He scraped along our car's offside wing and his body hit the front flat part of the caravan, throwing him off his bike.

An ambulance arrived and took the man to hospital. Our holiday was over, our caravan all smashed up and our car damaged though still, luckily, drivable. We headed straight back home, driving first to Ennis Caravans, where we bought the van. Luckily they specialised in rebuilding caravans, but it was several months before we saw it back.

That moment aside, we had some memorable times with it. I remember in Pembrokeshire parking on the cliff tops in a farmer's grass field, with a view of Skomer Island. Skomer ferry was just down the road, and we crossed to the island in it. That was an experience in itself, with rare birds all around. Landing on Skomer and walking round the island was even better, with puffins everywhere and chicks nesting just off our footpath with no apparent fear of humans.

At the same time, we began thinking of buying a new house. On some Sundays we would go around looking. One day we came across a small private development, twenty-seven two- or three-bedroom dormer houses being built in three small cul-de-sacs. They were all sold off plan, and there were about four or five remaining. We did our calculations; provided we could receive our expected price for our house, although being financially stretched, we could just manage it.

Our house went on the market with an asking price of £3,500. Remember we bought it for £2,400, so a gain of about £1,000. I thought 'Lovely jubbley'. We put it with a local Morriston estate agent whose manager was the owner. I liked that: we signed his normal contract and sat back. We looked in the local papers for the advert of our house then waited for viewings. We didn't get any. I wasn't a fan of his adverting style: he described the house as having 'valley views', which I reckoned would conjure up a view of old coal slag heaps. After several weeks, I visited him, discussed our situation, pointed out my opinion of 'valley views', and went home.

Several more weeks passed and nothing happened. I went back to him again, only this time I informed him I was going to try to sell it myself, that if he sold it I would pay him such fees that were in our contract but if I sold it he wasn't getting anything. He wasn't having this; he wanted his fees even if I sold it. We terminated the meeting; I thanked him then walked out. I put an ad in the paper myself.

I had a viewing on the first day: a young couple. They liked what they saw and said they would let me know. The following day the man rang back wanting his uncle to view with him. They came that very night. His uncle turned out to be a neighbour of ours, affectionately known to all as John the Bwllfa (the name of our road). I showed them around; John did much of the talking; it was evident he was here to negotiate a price. I offered him £100 off the asking price, which I had allowed for in our calculations, but he wanted another £100 off. I said no, they said thank you very much and that they'd let us know, and departed. Immediately after they left, I had a hurried discussion with Pat, saying 'I think I have made a mistake in letting them go.' Our house had been on the market a long time, and all depended on our completing this deal. Pat agreed; I swallowed my pride. Then, hurrying down the road after them, said we would accept their offer. We shook hands, the deal done.

We would visit our new house-to-be once a week, often in Pat's little green Morris Minor which we had picked up cheaply, handy for her to travel to work or do any shopping. The building of the house was going at a snail's pace, as there were others in front of us waiting for completion. Whilst our builder had a superb reputation for building good houses, he also had a reputation for being very difficult to deal with. However, eventually we moved in.

It was at about this time I started to take some private work on, as many colleagues were doing, though I think that in my contract of employment it was not permitted. It was what we call in Wales a hobble. I found it to be very lucrative. People would approach me on recommendation. I soon found another line, selling second-hand TVs. I would acquire a faulty set, refurbish it then sell it on.

BBC Wales, our main channel, first broadcast colour during July 1970. But there were very few colour sets about at the time, so our manager made the decision to appoint one engineer to service all colour sets. Lucky for me I got the job. I attended a one-week course on servicing colour sets at our head office in Swindon. I took the commitment with great pride, intending for our customers to receive the very best service possible.

Used colour sets were appearing in the market, as colour had first started in the UK during 1966. I started looking around for a supply, and found one at the small village of Stokenchurch, near High Wycombe. On my day off, I hired a van and drove there with cash in my pocket. I arrived at a warehouse: another cultural experience, for every Tom, Dick and Harry seemed to be trying to do the same as me. However, they did not seem to have a clue about what to buy or leave alone. I picked out about half-dozen sets, paid cash, said I'd be back, and left for the long drag back home.

My plan was that for every one I sold, I would invest the profits in another one. I would then rent out this second one. People would pay £6 a month for good, reliable colour TVs, and I reckoned I would be able to recoup my investment (in the first set) in six months, after which the income would be pure profit. (In fact, once the business got going, some of the sets lasted ten years – and were then usable for spares: a good chef wastes nothing. Lovely jubbly!)

As part of my planning I was also buying my own servicing test equipment – expensive items – and small second-hand van. This would mean that when I started up on my own I would have no additional expenses. I continued this for some time, then one day I was called in to our regional office and brought before our regional manager, whom I knew from his engineering days. It had come to his notice that I had been selling second-hand sets (there was no mention of rental). I told him I was doing the same thing as he had been doing when he was an engineer. He ignored that comment and told me in no uncertain terms that if I continued I would be sacked.

I gave what he said a lot of thought. My job was well paid, but… I thought, 'This is a crossroads for me. What do I do? To hell with him! He's not telling me what to do.'

It was my day off the following day. I had already hired a Luton van with the intention of travelling to Stokenchurch to buy a van-load of sets, so off I went.

I arrived to find there were only about half-dozen sets suitable. Terry, the owner with whom I had developed a good relationship, suggested I drive up to Birmingham, where he had another branch. He would telephone his chief engineer there who would prepare my order for my collection. As I was depending on this large consignment of sets to kick-start my business, I drove straight up to Birmingham, collected the sets, then drove straight back home, arriving around three in the morning. With Pat's assistance I filled my garage with them, grabbed a few hours' kip then returned the van, which had to be back early morning. So began my business.

Terry and I got on well, but we had the odd incident. One time I had arranged to pick up some sets. He came over to me and said that if I filled

At Stopsley school age 14.

As a young man.

Barry Island, with my mother and sisters.

Me organising a model railway exhibition on an open day at the school, just before I left at the age of 15 years old.

My Newport Harrier days with Des (left), a good 800 yards county standard runner, and Mike Rowlands (right), who ran the marathon twice for Wales, at the Commonwealth Games.

My mother in her youth.

Me taking a splash running cross country for Newport Harriers.

Third from the right, at Gan, the Maldives, with some RAF pals.

10 squadron bomber in flight.

My shop window at night.

Our first home in Penllergaer.

Before I could walk, with my dad, the photo cut in half.

Caroline in a school play, kneeling, front row. wearing most beads.

My squadron at square bashing, me centre row, far right.

Squadron 10 on the tarmac at RAF Butterworth, Malaysia.

The squadron again at Butterworth; our billets were the huts at the top of the picture.

Caroline at her graduation.

Our wedding day.

Happy days at Barry Island with my sisters.

On my 70th birthday birthday with my cousin Bram conquering the top of Pen y Fan.

*Pat and I in Hakaone National Park,
Mount Fuji in the distance.*

Disembarking at Mykonos, posers!

*Bomber Command
Memorial, Hyde
Park, Richard
wearing my father's
medals, Harrison
the miniature ones.
I felt nothing but
pride, so proud of
my dad. He was
lucky, his name
was not on the
memorial along
with the rest of the
brave men.*

My shop in its heyday, Gorseinon High Street. A shop of which I was proud.

As a corporal, RAF Cottesmore.

Having fun dune buggy riding in Cozumel.

More fun cross country buggy chasing.

At home in the winter.

Our peacful garden in the winter.

Looking from our gate down the road.

Chichen Itza, Mexico, a fantastic place.

Caroline's business venture, The Sloop Inn, which is 400 years old. Together we made it very smart, overlooking the picturesque banks of the River Wye, in the village of Llandogo.

Luxor and the Nile Valley, Egypt.

Our visit to the Mercedes factory, Stuttgart.

A long walk around Holy Islands, Northumberland.

At the top of Pen y Fan, on my birthday; it's great to be 70.

A fantastic day at Niagara, USA; notice that I still have my hat.

Now this guy thinks he's good, but I know someone who thinks he's better.

The best ladies on Wall Street.

Bram and I just before the assault on the Worm's Head, Gower coast.

Niagara again. What a smart hat. Emma's glasses are lush.

Under the cascades of Niagara.

Cracked it! At the top of the Worm's Head. Time for a cuppa.

Cartagena, Columbia
– emerald country.

A proud squadron at RAF Butterworth.
I am back row under the nose cone, fair
hair and no cap.

Richard's class at Ffynone House
School. He is second row thirrd from
left.

One of my dad's horses, Silent
Spring, breaking the track record
in the George Mason Haymarket
Trophy.

Finishing a large orienteering event at Pembrey.

Limbo dancing in Bermuda, courtesy of Panasonic. Rubber bones!

Orienteering through the silent forest.

Lucky dealers, on a 2-week Panasonic holiday to Japan. Pat is in the front row, I am fourth from the right just behind her left shoulder.

Number in Form	21.	Position in Form	14.
Punctuality	Good	Attendance	Good
Conduct	Good		

General Report on Work

Weakness in English is still a great drawback. He must make special efforts during the coming months to overcome this.

A.A.Brown. — Form Master/Mistress

— Head Master/Mistress

Parent's Signature — M. Kendrick.

Date — 16ᵗʰ July/54.

Name	Malcolm Kendrick		Form	3A.	
REPORT for	year		ending	July, 1954.	

GROUP	SUBJECT		REMARKS	TEACHER
Religious Educat'n		33	Satisfactory	A.A.B
English	Spoken English			
	Written Expression	38	Very weak indeed. Needs a greater effort.	G.W.J.
	Spelling	200		
	Literature			
	Reading			
Social Studies	History	52	Fair, English weak	G.W.
	Geography	53	Good	H.A.
Music		20	weak	
Science	General/Biology	37	Fair	
	Rural	55	Good	A.B
	Housecraft			
Mathematics		109 / 200	Has shown considerable improvement this term	A.A.
Tech. Drawing		90	Keen & has worked very well	P.J.D.
Physical Education			Excused.	John
Art and Craft	Art	80	Talentive	
	Craft	62	Good	
	Needlework			
	Woodwork	68	Fair	
	Metalwork			

Grading Code (where used) A=Excellent B=Above Average C=Average D=Below Average E=Weak

My school report – I bow my head in shame!

Caroline in the front row with the school tennis team.

Richard finishing second at Pembrey.

At ease on a swanky liner.

Richard, a winner of the Swansea Cubs Chess Tournament.

Winner of a Mitsubishi window competition.

Our Villa Caralino, Mijas Golf Course, Costa Del Sol.

*My grandmother
Daniels, who doted on
me. Unfortunately she
died not long after I was
born; had she lived my
life could have been very
different.*

Pat and I on our wedding day.

*Key guests at our wedding. They said, I would never get both my mother and
father to attend. I proved them all wrong, my Father, second from the left, my
mother standing far right.*

*Me at my trading desk.
Yes, same hat.*

Harrison, our little pride and joy, seeing his first train.

the van up he would give me a special reduced price. I had a quick look into the back of the van, estimated how many I could get in, and repeated to him, 'So I can take as many as the van will hold?' He said yes, and I shook hands with him, saying it was a deal. We started loading sets – but when the van was almost full, he turned and said, 'That's enough lads.' I looked at him and said, 'Hold on a minute, that was not the deal.' He gabbled on about how that was the deal. I turned around to his engineers and said, 'Right, lads, take them all off.' At this point the lads were all grinning behind his back, for Terry always had his own way. It must have taken him aback; he was about to lose two thousand pounds, and he quickly backed down to what he had originally agreed. I was annoyed with him, so I made sure we loaded up more than I estimated and then, to rub it in, I put one on the front seat.

However, we continued to do business together and he grew to trust me, as I always kept my word. He was a tremendous help to me, particularly if I wanted a colour tube, the most expensive item in the set (most of the tubes in the old sets were clapped out). He would sell me a tube for a tenner – a new one would be around £80. He would make sure I always had an almost new one.

I made one rule on commencing business, that I would only repair televisions I supplied. On my first day, I was out on a call at one of my customers, when I bumped into Tony, an engineer workmate of mine from Radio Rentals, who several months before me had also started a business in partnership with another person. Tony was building his business repairing sets. I had someone approach me for service, and gave him Tony's address for him to take the job. He thought I was nuts to only repair for my own customers, but I was on my own and knew I had to be very efficient. I only supplied colour televisions, which I now knew inside out, which made things quicker for servicing, as opposed to working with the huge range of black and white TVs, with which I was not familiar. Repairing these could be very time consuming, especially if they had an intermittent fault (you could never charge the customer for your time).

I gave myself two years to make the business work.

Chapter Twelve

Our Children, Caroline and Richard

I was keen to have children, but Pat wasn't. Eventually we agreed to have some. Unfortunately, Pat had gynaecological difficulties, and it looked like a child might not come. Then one day, about seven years after our marriage, Pat came home from work and announced that she was pregnant. We were both excited, as were Pat's mum and dad. They must have thought, 'About time too!', but as far as I can remember they had never hinted or pressurised us for grandchildren.

Then Pat was getting larger by the day, and then it was close to delivery time. One afternoon she said she was ready, and I drove her to Morriston Hospital, only about two miles away. Pat went into the delivery room; I waited in the corridor outside – in those days it wasn't normal for fathers to be present at delivery time (which suited me, as I didn't want to see all the gruesome details). I waited for what seemed hours, then late at night one of the nurses came to me saying, 'Come back in the morning'. I being clueless about babies went home, rose early next morning and drove straight to the hospital. Pat had not yet delivered. I hadn't seen her from when she first entered the ward. From being cool, I started to get concerned. I noted a little rushing about by nurses. I think they were saying the baby was in distress. Hearing that, so was I. Then a nurse came out announcing we had a baby girl. What a relief! I remember driving Pat home with the baby. She was so tiny that I was frightened to hold her for fear of hurting her.

Having yet to name her, we gave it some thought for a couple of days, then decided to name her Caroline Patricia Kendrick (born 07-10-1973).

Caroline came along lovely. She was a delightful toddler – I still remember holding her in my arms and singing Neil Diamond's 'Sweet Caroline' to her. In no time she was ready to start school. We arranged for her to begin at our village school in Penllergaer, where at the time a Mr Dennis was headmaster. Several days later Mr Dennis contacted us to say Caroline should not have started school, but he would allow her to continue. I was not happy with this, so we decided to make an appointment with Mrs Evans, the headmistress and owner of the prestigious, private Oakley House, near the centre of Swansea. Mrs Evans showed us around the well-kept, smart school, carefully observing Caroline at the same time and getting Caroline to read to her. At the end, she said she would take Caroline in. The fees would be £100 a term.

In this chapter, which is about my two children, I'm going to leap ahead of my own story, and tell theirs. The business that you saw me starting at the end of the last chapter was by now prosperous – I'll resume its narrative later – so we could now afford this.

Around this time, Pat became pregnant again. As she had had difficulty with having Caroline, they kept a much closer eye on her. They allowed me into the delivery ward to give her encouragement. I remember her wearing a hospital gown sitting on the floor with her back up against a wall, sweating, huffing, puffing, grumbling, mumbling – and telling me this was all my fault. I looked at her, half chuckling with a smile. If you say so… Every minute or so a nurse would come to see what was going on and telling her, 'Keep pushing, it's coming.' For the actual delivery, the nurse shoved me away – but very soon I was holding a baby boy. So different from last time! Pat wrapped him up in a shawl and we drove home, choosing for him the names Richard Malcolm Kendrick (born 9-5-78). He was christened at our local church.

Pat could devote her time to looking after him as I was now earning enough to maintain our family and keep Caroline in private school. Our children were happily growing up together. They would play safely within our little cul-de-sac, surrounded by green fields. There were other children of the same age around and they all had fantastic times together. When Richard came to the age of four, again we made an appointment with Mrs Evans and introduced her to Richard. She asked him what books he liked reading and he answered 'Encyclopaedias'.

Richard started at Oakley House. Pat would take them by car, about half an hour with heavy traffic, five days a week. At seven, Caroline moved on to Ffynone House School, a little more than a stone's throw from Oakley. Richard followed his sister there at the same age. Ffynone House is in an old rambling building, at the time taking in a little over 200 pupils, teaching them up to sixth form. The headmaster, Mr Rees Thomas, was the heart of the school. His previous employment had not been in education; he was charismatic, dynamic, full of energy, and inspired all around him. He was also a dab hand with the school plays, which all pupils got involved in.

The two began to show their individual personalities. Caroline would make friends easily. Richard was a quiet boy – though he had his friends – and was academically more gifted. Both had their extracurricular actives: Caroline, with speech and ballet; Richard with cricket and football. Caroline loved going to school and became centre of all that was happening socially.

Richard disliked going to school, but he was an obedient child and we never had a problem getting him there. When he was there he would give it his all. He had dyslexia, but the school dealt with this well. When it came to end-of-term exams, he was always top or thereabouts. There was another boy who started bullying him – not physically but emotionally. Richard told us, and I gave him a little lecture saying, 'Next time he bullies you, clench your fist but don't let him know. Then as quick as you can punch him straight on the nose as hard as you can, then he won't bother you again.' I was taking a gamble, for it might have triggered a mad streak in him, and if the school found out I would have been in trouble, too. I'm not one for violence, either, but I broke my own rule here. It worked: Richard never had any more trouble from the boy.

Caroline worked diligently for her O levels. To get into the sixth form, she would have to obtain five Cs or above. She got six, with some above

C, and entered the sixth form electing to study English Language, English Literature, and Art. She found the subjects difficult to master, but with encouragement from the staff plus us, stuck to it. Having passed her driving test at seventeen we bought her a little car, enabling her to make the school run on her own with Richard, taking the burden off Pat.

Meanwhile, Richard continued going from strength to strength. He and his friend Owen Talfan Davies would represent the school in debating competitions, making it to London for the national schools debating competition. Outside school, he and a number of his classmates joined Swansea Hockey Club, they all loved going there in the winter where they would be coached under floodlights. He also joined a local cricket club, and I would take him in the winter to Neath where Glamorgan coaches ran sessions for talented boys. He was proving to be an outstanding opening batsman, with a defence almost as good as Geoffrey Boycott's. I can remember on his fifteenth birthday taking him in the evening to play at St Helens, Swansea, the famous cricket ground where one-day internationals were played. Swansea had the pick of youngsters; it was the club they all wanted to play for. Our local village team, Ynystawe, were playing them in an area league 20-over youth match. He opened with his usual partner Darrel, and they between them had an opening partnership of 100, in which Richard hit his first six, a straight drive over the bowler's head out of the ground into St Helens road. Not many can claim to have accomplished that on their fifteenth birthday.

The next game taught a less positive lesson. It was midweek knock-out cup game against a local valley side who we knew would not present to much of a challenge for us. Richard and I arrived at the ground to find that Richard had been put down the order to bat at seven. The decision had been made by the father of a batsman who played for the county. I took Richard to one side, telling him that we would say nothing and he should let his bat do the talking. I still refer to that incident, when he has other problems in life. Cricket at schoolboy level has so much nepotism, it's sad to say.

Caroline became hockey captain at the school. She wasn't the best player – a couple played for the county – but she sorted other sides out. When they played state schools, where some players thought they could bully these namby pamby private school types, Caroline, from her position at left back, would give them a mouthful every bit as strong as her side got. Her coach, who had played for Wales over 50 times, recognised her character. She became deputy head girl – it was rumoured at the time that she would have been made head girl, but there was one girl destined for Oxbridge and it would look good on her CV.

She sat her A levels and applied to a number of places for further study. The best offer came from a London polytechnic: if she got three Cs, she could have a place on a degree course reading hotel management. When her results came through she was disappointed – three grade Es. But she didn't give up. She went to Cardiff Institute of Higher Education instead, taking the same degree as at the London polytechnic (she ended up passing with a 2-1, a fine achievement).

At the same time, the more academic Richard got cracking results in his GCSEs, 11 of them, all C or above, with A grades in Biology, English Lit, French, Geography, German, Maths, and A* grades in History and Physics. Not bad for someone who is dyslexic! For doing so well in his exams we bought him a car having passed his driving on his seventeenth birthday.

Richard wanted to leave Ffynone House, preferring to attend Gorseinon Sixth Form College, very local to us. Pat and I let him do so, knowing he would be walking into a different culture than private school – this would introduce him into the real world, an education in itself. I remember dropping him off at the school gates, with him not knowing a single person at this large school. He said, 'Dad, don't come up with me. I will go on my own.' I felt very proud at that moment.

Richard chose to study Geography, Maths and Physics for A level. Actually, the school wasn't as difficult as we feared: once students move into the sixth form most of the trouble-makers have been left behind. Richard quickly made many friends, including his wife-to-be, Emma. Study-wise, he was not as attentive as he should have been, particularly with his Physics teacher, Mr Sykes, who he would clash with. His predicted grades were two Cs with a B in Maths, but just before the exams he decided to focus and work for a better result. He wanted to read Engineering at university and applied to top universities (not Oxbridge, where he didn't want to go. Gorseinon College was keen that he attend the group who were being groomed for this. I asked him why he didn't want to join them and his answer was that they were all eggheads, focusing their whole life on Oxbridge). One of the places he applied for was Cardiff University, which was listed as number one for Engineering (though this was not the reason he choose it; he said to me he wanted to go because the social life at the students' union was the best!). He had an offer from Bristol, which I would have preferred, but turned it down.

On the morning of the Maths exam he had a massive migraine, something Pat always has under stress. We were not going to send him in for the exam, but I telephoned the school and explained the situation. They said we should send him and they would keep a close eye on him. All went well. He passed with A in Geography, A in Physics and B in Maths. So off he went to where he wanted, Cardiff.

Outside Gorseinon College, he had many learning experiences. I started him with a Saturday job in my shop during the holidays, delivering and installing TV equipment. On the sports field he continued to excel. He started his own basketball club with his friends, going on to win a local competition. Perhaps his best achievement was playing cricket in the final of a knock-out competition against Dafan, a side that included two fast bowlers who where both playing for Wales under 17s. The Ynystawe coach decided not to open the batting with his normal two openers, Darrel and Richard, choosing instead to open with Darrel and Richard Gordon, a prolific, free-scoring batsman. I didn't think this was right against such pace bowlers – and Gordon was out in the first over. Richard came in at number three. Darrel was out the next over. Ynystawe were in trouble. If Richard's wicket were to fall, I feared that would have been the end. However, Richard was never one to panic. He stood up strong and resolute to these two fast bowlers, who in an attempt to get him out started to bowl beamers at him (that's when they bowl the ball directly at your upper body). Both bowlers were warned they would be taken off if it continued. Wickets continued to fall rapidly. The team was eight wickets down when their allocated number of overs came to an end. Richard was still in. He'd scored less than 30 runs, but as he walked from the wicket to the pavilion he received a standing ovation from both sides. One of the bowlers was Simon Jones, who went on to become a successful fast bowler for England, helping them to regain the Ashes in the famous 2005 series (his father was Jeff Jones, who regularly played for England in the 1960s). Richard's claim to fame would be that

Simon Jones couldn't get him out: there's not many can say that. The Duke of Wellington reputedly said that the Battle of Waterloo was won on the playing fields of Eton; I say Richard's Waterloo was won on the cricket pitch at Ynystawe.

Pat and I drove him up to Cardiff University for his first term. We were only 50 miles away so he could come home regularly. He settled down to his degree, which he completed successfully in July 2000, gaining first class honours. Richard decided that there was little money to be made in engineering, so he applied to companies with better earning potential. The first interview he attended was at Price Waterhouse Coopers, who turned him down. Most of the big investment banks did the same without even giving him an interview, all except one.

They offered him a job as a graduate trainee. We were over the moon. In his intake there were 36 graduates; the course was to be three months, after which they would have a choice of which department they would enter. Each department would only take one on, and he said, 'Dad, there's only one department I would like to go in to, that's risk management, but there's a chap from Cambridge with a PhD in Maths applying for that one too.' I replied that this was a tough one, but he should put his name down anyway. He got the job.

He shared a flat with a friend, Ross, who had been at Cardiff with him, and who had got a first, too. Needless to say they were also drinking mates. But he wanted a place of his own. I travelled up to London for two days, staying with Caroline, who at that time had a flat in Croydon, and looked at loads of places. In the last one, a new two-bedroom flat right by the River Thames, the sales person showed me around a concrete skeleton – that's all it was except for a show flat on the ground floor. I thought, 'super, this is just what Richard wants' and telephoned him at work, asking if could get over at 5.30pm, which was when the sales office closed.

He could. We walked up through the concrete rubble on the stairs, reaching the fourth floor and the skeleton that was to be the flat, and spent some time visualising what the aspects would be. Both of us were sold on it; in my mind I made some quick calculations to see if it was financially possible. It was, so we went ahead and bought it. When it was finished, Emma joined him. She got a job as a radiographer with a private practice in Harley Street.

Richard continued with his bank, obtaining a transfer to New York, allowing him to further his career by working on Wall Street. In 2005 he was appointed a vice president. We were so pleased; he had been a loyal employee and had worked exceptionally hard. Two years later, he returned to London. At the age of 36, he became appointed as a managing director, responsible for worldwide risk asset management.

While all this was going on, Caroline had completed her degree and taken up a graduate trainee job with a national company with a chain of three-star hotels. She started in Birmingham; after around six months her employer acquired another hotel not far away with its own grounds, a little bit more upmarket than their normal offering, and she was appointed assistant manager. The manager was more often than not absent, leaving Caroline in charge. It was always short of staff; she would complain to the regional manager whom she knew well, but nothing was ever done about it. Eventually she just walked out – I was angry with her, saying she should have found another job first.

However, she is not one to let the grass grow under her feet. She found a job with Regus, who rent office space. They were relatively small at the time but rapidly expanding nationally. They employed her as an assistant branch manager.

I discussed with her about buying a flat in London, but her salary was not very high. However, if we bought a flat and she shared it with someone, that would pay half the mortgage for her. I kicked around some figures in my head. She decided on West London near the M4 motorway allowing easy access to London but with a good connection to come home in Wales, as she wished. I scoured the press for properties within her range, decided to visit about half-dozen, and gave it a day for my initial visit. I drove up first thing one morning, visiting my first estate agent. On his books he had, on a private estate in Yiewsley, a fairly new small two-bedroom flat on the top floor of a four storey building. There was plenty of green space, maintained by a management company, and allocated car parking. A charming canal ran along one side of the estate. I checked the time of the walking distance to the station: four minutes. Super, I thought; this could be the property to gauge others by. I saw five others before returning home to Swansea, but none came up to the first. I arranged for the estate agent to show Caroline around; she and I met up there; she liked what she saw and decided to buy it.

She became unsettled at Regus, and noted in the national press that a position was going as a guest relations manager with Holiday Inn Hotel, Mayfair, their flagship hotel at the time. She got an interview and was given the job, which involved overseeing all the staff training. She made a very good friend there, Mark (the relationship was purely platonic). When she worked on a weekend she would book Pat and myself in at an attractive staff rate. Dinner was especially good; she would make sure the chef made it extra special for us. The ambiance was super relaxing: a live grand piano playing softly in the background, widely spaced out dining tables with sumptuous high back easy chairs with wings; well presented, attentive and relaxing staff – what more could you wish for?

She had ambitions to own her own business, however. She fancied a pub offering accommodation. I thought the best way was to go for freehold, where one had the freedom of choice and wasn't beholden to landlords. I looked at pubs around the Home Counties, South East England, South Wales and the Border Counties. I became quite a dab hand at assessing pubs, even though I only had the occasional glass of wine in each one. Most were out of my price range (I was backing this project for her). Finally, I found one within budget, with potential to develop (we did not want one that was already working to its full capacity). The Sloop Inn nestled in the Wye Valley, a little more than a stone's throw from the river itself, on the main A466 road through the green village of Llandogo. It had been built in 1707, as a cider house. A mountain stream ran through its cellars – good for keeping the cellars cool but difficult to handle with torrential rain. It was in poor condition, only just viable financially, and had been on the market for some considerable time. But... On the back of the ground floor was a large room, very dated and grotty, but with large windows overlooking the Wye. Great potential for a dining room. The bar room had old fashioned beams, supported by huge sections of tree trunks: a mass of character but in lousy condition. The B&B accommodation offered three double and one single room, accommodation for a chef, plus a self-contained one-bedroom flat for the owner. It had its own car park on the opposite side of the road. Caroline came to look at it, then we went home to consider the purchase. We decided to go for it, and applied to the bank for a loan. They approved and we bought it.

It meant Caroline selling her flat in Yiewsley, which was sad (the flat had doubled in price whilst she owned it, which softened the blow). We gutted the large dining room, and Caroline designed a new one. New furniture, new carpets, plus anything else that needed doing: I did much of the physical work, helping a local builder. When finished, it proved to be a lovely place to dine. We also carried out work on the outside of the building, making it more attractive looking, sprucing the car park up, redecorating the flat and the letting rooms, refurbishing the bar. All was within budget.

The venture proved to be a disaster; I don't think Caroline realised the amount of commitment involved: it was a 24/7 job. There were endless difficulties employing chefs, cleaners and part-time staff. Most wanted under-the-counter payments, but we were not prepared to do this. There were problems with absenteeism. Eventually she took over the chef's job herself, as she was qualified. She was also doing the cleaning and making all the bedrooms up herself after guests had gone, as cleaners would not turn up.

I would come up for the day once a week to do her books for her, and offer any advice I could, but after a year she had had enough. We put the pub on the market with the same national commercial property marketer we had bought it from. Pubs were now closing nationally at an alarming rate, and there were ones everywhere for sale. However, we had a good set of books and the place looked lovely. We upped the price from our purchase price to one where we could get all our investment back plus a small profit. The key negotiator, an experienced salesman, wanted us to price it at £50k less. I said, 'No, put it on at our figure.' We quite quickly had a couple of show-rounds, then out of the blue we had one with someone who had no idea about the industry but wanted a pub. He liked the place and came back with an offer £10k less than the asking price. In the past, he had tried to buy pubs and had been gazumped. I said, 'Give us the asking price and we will agree not to gazump you.' The deal was completed. By Jove, was I relieved; we had got out of jail free and actually shown a profit.

While all this was going on with Caroline, Richard and Emma decided to tie the knot in 2007. They came back to Wales for the marriage, choosing the boutique Hurst House Hotel, Laugharne, a village associated with the

Welsh poet Dylan Thomas and his boat house, where he lived the last four years of his life. The hotel had fantastic views over the River Taf estuary. The wedding was a grand occasion, with all our families together. Nick, his best friend from school, was the best man, and Caroline the chief bridesmaid. Some of Richard's American friends flew over for the event. Emma looked lovely in a white wedding dress.

On moving back to London, Richard decided to sell his flat in the Canary Wharf district, and buy a property near his workplace at Saint Paul's, where he could walk to work. He discovered a three-storey two-bedroom modern mews-style house, within a gated development of 12 houses, built by a private developer, which had direct access to the canal at Islington. It would cost him more than double the price he sold his old one for – but he was doing well in the City.

Later, he decided that he wanted to live even closer to his work, as he could be on call much of the time. As usual he fully researched the market, and found a company that was building a new development at Saint Bartholomew's Square. The square was vibrant with cafés and bars; the development had its own secluded courtyard garden tucked away at the rear – as well as a five-star concierge service, its own residents' lounge and cinema and underground garage space. He bought off plan, and was now able to walk to his office several hundred yards away.

Caroline departed from The Sloop Inn with all her belongings to a new house she had bought near Swansea, on the Gower Coast above the village of Penclawydd. It had tremendous views over the wide Loughor estuary to Burryport in the distance, and a large long rear garden backing onto green grazing fields with a stile to access them. There were three bedrooms, a conservatory and an enormous lounge.

She was now looking in earnest for a job within the hospitality industry, the one she knew best, applying to most of the best hotels in the area. She was shocked by how little knowledge some of the managers had of the hotel business. At one five-star place, her interviewer seemed to know nothing about hotels at all. She was offered a job on a ridiculously low wage, so the person could pick her brains.

Instead, she cast the net wider and took a job with a very small wage but incentives on a high commission basis, which entailed telephoning medical practices and selling locum doctors to them for short-term cover. It wasn't long before she was hitting her targets and more; eventually she became the leading sales person, taking most of the work that came in, while the rest were sitting around doing next to nothing. The owner of the business then called a meeting of all sales staff, in which she announced a change of rules. She intended sharing Caroline's commission amongst all the staff. Caroline stood up, walked out of the job and decided to start her own business in competition with them, operating it by herself from the spare bedroom at her house. This continued successfully for a number of years, then suddenly it all dried up, the National Health Service deciding to channel the business through a few selected large organisations.

She started looking around for a job. She answered an ad in the local newspaper for a job as a mortgage advisor, had an interview, then was offered a job as a trainee. She asked me what I thought of the package offered, and I told her she was not playing to her strengths, but to her weaknesses, maths, and that she shouldn't take it. How wrong I was. On the practical side of selling she was brilliant, and she battled through the nine-month course before passing the national examination to become a mortgage advisor. She was over the moon, as we were.

She now had a baby to look after, as, while living at Penclawydd, she started living with a man she had met but whom Pat and I did not approve of and became pregnant by him. We all loved the baby, Harrison, however – our first grandchild. Caroline continues to this day as an independent mortgage advisor, part of a firm based in Newport, earning much more than she would ever have been paid working for someone else in the hospitality industry.

Before I move on I will tell my version, worked out through my own experience, of the story we all know of the Tortoise and the Hare. My son Richard is a hare – but a smart one. He always does just enough and no more. Caroline is a smart tortoise – as I think I am. We lack the hares' natural speed, but throughout life we will pass many a hare, never to see them again. The moral of this tale is that a smart hare will always beat a tortoise, even a smart one, but either will beat an unwise hare.

CHAPTER THIRTEEN
STARTING MY OWN BUSINESS

Back to the narrative...

Starting out on my own was the biggest business decision I ever made. I was risking all. But having planned everything out in my mind, I was confident that I would not fail. In fact, failing never entered my head. As already stated, I had laid down the foundations of my business before leaving Radio Rentals and had calculated that in the worst case scenario I could survive for two years. I knew it was going to be tough, but I was never frightened of work.

The business grew, and the time came when it became too large to operate from my house. I made the decision to buy a shop. I had no intention of leasing or renting one, lining someone else's pockets, and approached my bank for assistance with this. There were no problems, and I was clear to search for a property within my budget. I had no intention of selling my own house and buying a shop with a flat above, as some people recommend. I wanted Pat and our children to maintain a good quality of life outside of work.

I scoured the area, and decided to buy one on the high street of our local small town of Gorseinon, around two miles from where we were living. The shop was in a terraced row, and not being used as a shop but as a house. It was in a rundown state, so I had a look around it with a local builder, with whom I discussed what needed doing and the costs. I made an offer; it was accepted, so I became the owner.

I named my business Kendrick Colour: the word colour was fashionable at the time for television shops. I did not form a limited company, a bit naive perhaps, but I never intended not to settle a debt. Looking back now at the size I grew to, perhaps it would have been better for me.

I had one competitor of any consequence, Lewis's TV, who happened to be the largest independent rental company in South Wales. I made the decision not to clash with them, but to do things my own way. Any make he stocked, I would not. As luck would have it he had just done an exclusive deal with Decca, and also withdrawn from the South Wales buying group, so this allowed me a free hand on my choice of manufacturer. I jumped into the buying group, thus effectively keeping Lewis's out.

While the shop was being prepared, I approached National Panasonic, as they were known at the time, for a dealership. I remember it clearly as if it were yesterday, meeting their regional manager, Peter Ruck, with whom I eventually built up an excellent working relationship, sitting on a bench on a sunny day, discussing my dealership application. I don't think he was too impressed to start with, as I recall him initially suggesting I apply in the future when I had settled in. However, I managed to persuade him otherwise. I was allocated the dealership. I also signed up with Mitsubishi, who made the most reliable TV sets ever, though they only offered two models and were priced the highest of all TV manufacturers. I also secured a dealership from Rank Radio, whose brand was Murphy. *Déjà vu*! I had now gone full circle; my first job offer was with Murphy at Welwyn Garden City.

When the shop was finished, I moved in. I was now on my own doing everything from sales, servicing, rebuilding TVs, to going to Stokenchurch for scrap sets to rebuild – though Pat started doing the rental collection from metered sets. I opened the shop quietly, with no advertising or any of the normal funfair or fuss. It was rumoured that my competitor said, 'He won't be there long; I have seen them all come and go.'

I just carried on about my business. It was an eye opener to find the retail selling side such a cut-throat business. There was one retailer on Swansea High Street with a fantastic display of every conceivable make, shown off to its best, on sale on wafer-thin margins – but offering a service that was at the other end of the scale to his display. There would be customers standing outside his shop with placards detailing their complaints. I just carried on selling with my mark up on price, emphasising our service that was prompt, expert and personal.

It was lucky I had the rentals business, as in that first year I sold very little. The rentals went from strength to strength. I would finance personally all the rental sets I bought, including new Panasonic TVs. By contrast, many others would be in 'partnership' with someone like Phillips. They would sign a contract with the manufacturer for, say, 50 sets, to repay the cost of the sets plus fancy interest, back over two years, after which the set became the property of the dealer. I got my money back after one year, and the sets were mine from day one.

The business soon became too much for me to handle on my own. I now had over 200 sets out on rental. I wanted to employ an engineer who could share the load with me. This is where I had a trump card that many others did not have: I knew a good engineer from a bad one. I also knew just the person for the job, someone I had worked with at Radio Rentals when he started work as a young lad, and to whom I had spoken about joining me before leaving. Dave Ellis lived locally in Gowerton, about 3 miles from the shop. He started with me, relieving the workload no end. We got on like a house on fire – for a long time, anyway.

I was becoming recognised as a local pillar of society; people knew they could trust me to my word. I was also understanding of the poor, of which there were many in Gorseinon. If they had a meter on their set, I would let them fall into arrears until they could sort their affairs out – sometimes waiting for over a year. I built a considerable amount of respect during the Scargill/Thatcher miners' strike. When miners came in to say they couldn't pay, I would say, 'Leave it, I can wait until you are on your feet again.' Most of these people are the salt of the earth; as far as I can remember, every single miner honoured their debt in the end.

The business continued to grow, with people coming to buy from us from all over the district. Kendrick Colour had an upmarket image, supplying the best quality goods, with the owner's personal attention and first class repair service. The shop became too small for our needs and I had now cleared the bank of any loans for it. Next door was a double-fronted property with an extension at the back. It was occupied by a local carpet firm and used to store carpets, and was in a state of poor repair – it needed gutting to be suitable for us. Although not openly on the market, I knew by word of mouth that the owner would sell. I approached him, and he agreed to sell – then came back to me to say someone else was now interested in buying, so the price had gone up – in other words, he gazumped me. Normally at this point I would walk away from the deal, and say, 'Even if you come back to me with the original agreed price, I still won't buy.' But this deal was by far the best for me. By now I had acquired a little bit of wisdom, so I swallowed my pride and bought the property on his terms.

I stripped the ground floor out, converting the premises into a modern, carpeted up-market shop. I installed a new shop front with two large windows looking straight into the showroom, large protruding shades over the windows and a huge illuminated sign across the whole of the front of the building. We moved out of next door, which I had no trouble selling for around twice the price I paid for it. I took on a new employee, Martin, a young chemist who had been made redundant. He had no experience of sales or electronics, but he impressed me so I took him on. He turned out to be a terrific salesman and totally trustworthy.

It was the dawn of the satellite age. Were we in on it? You bet we were. I contacted someone who was on the cutting edge of dish installations. He installed for me a 2-meter spun aluminium dish, the best available at the time, erected in the shop's back garden. The regional manager of Salora arranged for us to have a trailer with a satellite dish mounted on top parked outside the shop front – luckily we had an exceptionally wide pavement. We connected up one of Salora's latest satellite sets in the shop to show off to customers. It proved to be a great success, not so much as to how many of them we sold – they were expensive and the instructions were all in Russian – but in building our image as a firm who knew what they were doing. No other dealer in the district had anything like this.

The business continued to grow. Dave and I were now stretched on the engineering side, and my engagement with customers grew. I decided to employ another engineer and approached Stan Dixon, a top engineer I had been friendly with when working for Radio Rentals. He was still working there, but had a medical problem with depression, which caused him to need large stretches of time off. Stan and I had a chat. I showed him around the shop and our workshops, explained what we were all about. Stan, when in an upbeat mood, was a bubbly sort of person, always joking and laughing. He was chubby, with a fussy hair cut and a short beard: if we wanted a Father Christmas in for Christmas, Stan would be the ideal man.

He was very enthusiastic about it all, so thinking I could keep him from his depressions by keeping him happy, I invited him to join us. Dave was now service manager, but they knew each other well and worked together as a team. From this point on I would do no more servicing unless we were desperate. Running the business had now become a full time occupation. We now had two of our own small vans on the road. I never believed in renting vans; I would buy a van and run it to the ground, by far the most cost-effective way, and good advertising too, as it had Kendrick Colour plastered all over it.

The shop workload was increasing, too. I employed a series of shop assistants. Normally they wouldn't be with me very long before moving on, but I also had some very good lads, who lasted longer.

In 1977 I was privileged to be invited by Panasonic to a presentation of a new consumer device: a video recorder. I had never seen one before, and remember the presentation as clearly as if it were today. We sat and watched a TV screen, on which a video was shown where a girl in a red swimsuit held a large red rubber ball in front of herself and bobbed and jiggled around to the rhythm of background music. The psychology worked; it kept the all-male audience's eyes glued to the screen. Panasonic were not bringing many into the country before Christmas, and they would be on allocation and priced at a little over £1,000. The maximum I would be allowed was 10. I was impressed and ordered my ten. By Christmas they had all gone at the full price – I gave no discount, but as usual we would install the video and set it up for no charge, plus give free service calls for the length of the guarantee. We were the first in the area to sell video recorders; other dealers were scared off by the high price. I remember one dealer I knew who was chairman of the buying group I belonged to saying to me, 'You had a killing this Christmas!' So I did, but he had the same chance. Did he have any bottle? Doesn't look like it…

As with colour televisions, the introduction of video recorders soon brought every Tom, Dick and Harry onto the bandwagon. There were video recorder shops opening all over the place. I remember one opening opposite a central roundabout in the middle of Swansea. It looked a very nice shop, selling all makes and all formats, with the usual 'All at discount prices! We won't be beaten!' promotion. The owner purported to be an expert, having a column in the local rag, giving talks on the local radio – but he seemed to know little about how video recorders actually worked. Most of Joe public were taken in by it, and we lost many sales to this outlet, but I kept to my policy on price – plus if you didn't buy it from us we wouldn't service it.

I wasn't in business at the start of colour television rentals, but now I was in at the very start of video recorder rentals. I opted to rent and sell the VHS format only, as I considered it the best on the market. I had a good relationship with the manufacturers, for whom I was a favoured dealer: they would look after me when supplies were short.

I was also selling recorders. There was a lot of hire purchase through me to a national finance company. I decided to cut this middleman out and formed my own company, Figurewise Ltd. I could take on riskier customers than a large company would. I realised there would be losses through this policy which I tried to build into the structure of the loans. If people did default, I would not use a solicitor – expensive – but make my own claim through the small claims' court and represent myself.

It was about this time I had a situation with Dave, the first person I'd employed. I was in the office one lunchtime needing to do some paper copying. I went over to the copier, lifted the top, and there, on the glass inside was a rental contract of mine. I never had contracts photocopied, I had them printed by a printer. Thinking this was odd, I looked at the contract and saw that Dave had doctored one of my contracts for his own needs with his own particulars on. He was running his own rental business on the side. I felt both annoyed and sad. I waited until he came back after lunch and tackled him about it. After our chat, I said, 'Dave, go away and think about it.' He came back the next morning and handed his notice in.

I was relived, for I didn't have to make the inevitable decision. He started up in Gowerton, the next small village to me, effectively in competition. I think he struggled for a couple of years then closed down. I made Stan service manager, which was in some ways better for me. Dave had been a quiet type, while Stan would chat engagingly to anyone.

I advertised for an engineer to replace Dave. I had never advertised for an engineer before. It turned out to be quite an experience. I was not short of applicants and wasn't going to spend a vast amount of time interviewing people, so I turned half down before the interviews. Some of the people I interviewed turned out to have had real cheek to even apply. I would start with some difficult technical questions, then if they didn't know the answer I would move on to something less demanding, and so on, until I arrived at their level. In some cases they didn't even know Ohm's Law. Others who had their full City and Guilds Certificate in Colour Engineering thought they knew all the answers but weren't so smart when I started talking practical detail. Others did have the knowledge, but came over as smart arses. In the end I chose Lewis Williams, who had served his time learning the trade at Thomas Brothers of Llanelli (Dave, the owner, was a good business friend of mine: a fellow Panasonic dealer, we would help each other with stock when short).

Lewis was a very quiet and shy person and started working alongside Stan. Being engineers, their minds worked very much the same and they got on well. Lewis proved to be a fine engineer.

I started a video library to encourage customers to buy video recorders. With the sale of a recorder I would offer free membership and, as a further incentive, the first five video rentals free. I searched the market for a good supplier of recorded video tapes. There was one in London which had been established for some time. Stan and I drove up one day and picked out around 150 tapes, and that was our library started. It went well to start with, but soon there were video rental shops popping up everywhere. They would cut prices to a minimum. They would copy tapes then rent them out: these were rubbish quality and caused dirty video heads – for which they sold, as a remedy, head cleaning tapes which if used too often damaged the head and made a replacement necessary. However, the average Joe public did not care until they had a problem and came in banging on the counter.

A video rental shop opened up three doors down from my shop, a really grotty place, hoping to pick business off the back of me, no doubt. Any profit I expected to make with this line was now gone, the only use it had now was as a marketing tool: I had no intention of competing with him.

Panasonic invited me and around another fifty dealers for a week's holiday in Bermuda, gusted by the UK managing director, Mr Imura, who first brought Panasonic to the UK. We stayed at the Southampton Princess, now known as the Fairmont Southampton, surrounded by its own golf course, paradise-like empty white beaches a stone's throw away. It was a dream holiday for Pat and myself: full board and everything laid on for us, including evening entertainment. I remember one evening having a limbo dance competition where everyone was expected to join in. Guess who won it? No, not me, but Mr Imura. By Jove, he was old rubber bones and could get under a foot. I was chuffed to come third; these days I'd be lucky to go under five feet!

Video cameras were now being launched by Panasonic. We started to sell them in the selling season between September and Christmas. They were popular. They were expensive items which ensured a good profit, providing of course you could get the stock. I ensured this by getting my orders in at the manufacturers' shows in London. Each manufacturer took space at one of the posh five-star hotels. This was known as the Radio Show, a name taken from the 1950s when the show was under one roof at Earl's Court. I remember going there several times when around sixteen or seventeen, with my mates from college who were on the radio course with me. I remember the first launch of the first all transistor portable radio, in 1957, by a new firm on the block: Perdio, a British company. It was the talk of the show. Now I was not going as an insignificant young lad, but as a dealer who would be wined and dined by all. I would be accommodated for my night's stay, by Mitsubishi at the five-star Portman Hotel, by Panasonic at the Copthorne Tara, Kensington, where I always received flattering treatment from them. Panasonic's manager Peter Ruck would spend considerable time with me showing all the latest products that were about to be introduced. He would fill his order book up with my requirements for the run-up to Christmas. I knew that if I didn't order now, there would be little chance of getting anything otherwise, unless it was through cancellations.

Mitsubishi were extending their product range in the UK, too. They increased the range of their televisions and brought in hi-fi, video recorders and a large screen colour projection television. I would stock all these items, so we effectively became the focal point in the area for Mitsubishi.

The large screen projector, which at the time cost mega-bucks, I placed in the middle of our shop window. It became an attraction, increasing the shop's already upmarket image, though I never sold many. Everybody wanted a discount, but I had my bottom line and would not go under that.

On every January the first I would draw up a large graph, around 3ft square, projecting the sales for the forthcoming year based on past results. I would then hang it on the office wall. Over the years, it proved an excellent indication of how the business was doing. One time, at the height of the boom years, I had to stick an extra sheet of graph paper on the top to accommodate the extra growth.

Chapter Fourteen

The People Side of Business

The people you work with can make or break your business. Here are some stories, good and bad.

Family made a huge contribution, always ready to do their bit. Pat kept the books up to date and would collect from our meter rental boxes. After the sudden death of her husband, I gave my mum a Saturday job helping in the showroom; it took her mind off her loss and helped her finances. She was also a great source of information on the goings-on behind my back. I think she felt proud of me for what I had achieved. I have already mentioned that Richard worked for me occasionally, installing televisions, VCRs and hi-fi for me. He never came back from a job saying he couldn't do something; sometimes he would telephone me asking about some problem he was having, but he always sorted it out.

But you can't just work with family.

It was always very important to me to make Kendrick Colour a pleasant place to work.

I was successful in this most of the time, and we lost very few people.

Apart from the story of Dave, above, I only ever had to dispose of two senior members of staff. The first one was Bill, a salesman I had known from my Radio Rentals days. As he lived a long way away, I let him take one of our vans home with him, on the understanding that he wouldn't use it for private use. A little while later I had a report that the van was seen travelling around Swansea. I hauled him into my office and gave him a rollicking, telling him in no uncertain terms that if he did it again I would take the van off him. Within two days I had reports of him beeing seen driving around. I had him in the office again and just said, 'Bill, you can't take the van home again.' From then on, he got a lift into work from his wife, but was always moaning and groaning about it.

I then found that he was not such a brilliant salesman. Several weeks after the van incident, he was installing a new television for one of our existing customers, an old lady, who could be vulnerable to con men. The next morning she telephoned up saying the set wasn't right. I sent Stan down the same day to sort it out; he came back saying that the scan coils were twisted, which meant that the picture had been on a slant. Bill had solved this problem by putting a book under one side of the set!

I called Bill over and asked for an explanation; he gave me some cock and bull story. I don't employ people I don't trust, so sacked him on the spot, telling him I would send him his week's pay at the end of the week. I then called upstairs to Stan to take Bill home; he had no transport, so that was the kindest thing I could do.

I also had to get rid of my first showroom manager. He impressed me greatly at interview, with his credentials and mannerisms. He said he was a member of Mensa, and a preacher who on Sundays would travel around various chapels preaching the gospel. He pushed for more money than I was offering, but I liked him so we compromised and I took him on. I spent around a week with him in the showroom showing him how we functioned, then let him get on with his job. To start with, sales were good. But slowly I noted a change.

Pat and I were sitting at our desks (she would come in on an ad hoc basis to do her bookkeeping), and he came into the room to enquire about something, then, as he was going out turned to me and said, 'You can't afford me.' I looked across at Pat and said nothing, but logged it in my mind. I then kept an eye on him at his work, and noticed that he was giving customers the impression that he owned the shop. Sales stayed good, however, so I let it be.

'Mr Mensa' as I shall call him could turn his hand to all sorts of practical things. For example, one winter in the run-up to Christmas, I had agreed with Mitsubishi to fit one half of the showroom out with new swanky ceiling-to-floor wall stands, and with Panasonic to do the same for the other half. The purchase cost of the gear would be split 50/50, but the makers of the stands offered to fit them at a fancy price. I decided we would install them ourselves. Mr Mensa got this done for us. Brilliant. But then I found out that he had told the staff they could have an extra day off – at our busiest time of year.

I said I wanted to speak to him about this and he agreed to do so at the end of the day. When that came, I noticed none of the staff had left. He told me that I should speak to 'all of us'. He held his arms out wide and gather everyone together to beckon them all. The penny dropped.

I told him that if he had anything to say to me, he could come up to my office, and that this applied to everyone in the business: it was always open to them.

Having effectively stirred up a mutiny, he had to go. He came up to my office and I 'let him go'.

Then the showroom staff handed their notices in, too, all except for one lad, Peter.

This included Ian, a sales assistant who had been with me from leaving school at sixteen and who was starting to develop into a good salesman of electrical goods. Sadly, he was the sort of person that could be easily led. He got a job as a barman in a village pub; six months later he came into the shop and admitted he had made a mistake leaving. Lewis handed his notice in, too. I had a very long talk with him, explaining what Mr Mensa was up to, and persuaded him to stay by offering him the job of service manager and giving him a massive pay rise. I also said, 'Lewis, you watch. The atmosphere here will change.' A couple of weeks later he came up to me and said, 'Malc, you were right. The atmosphere has changed back to the way it was before this guy arrived.'

(I am not impressed by Mensa, by the way. Because Richard was academic, we had him tested by them – they send you the test by post and you send it back to them. His results came back as 'average'. This actively discouraged him for a while. But he then went back to excelling at school and getting a first at university. Average?)

Someone once approached me offering to be a freelance salesman, with his own transport. It sounded impressive and I felt I had nothing to lose, so I decided to give him a trial with a couple of TVs. His pitch was that he would visit the council houses up in the valleys, offering to sell sets paid for over two years. I would pay him an agreed commission for each sale. He came back the following day with the agreements all signed and correct. I allowed him more sets, and in next to no time he had agreements for fifty sets.

Was it too good to be true? Dave, Stan and I made some visits to the homes where the salesman said he had rented the sets, and heard very different stories about the deal these people had thought they were getting. Next morning he breezed into my office, asking for more sets. I quietly told him that I was dispensing with his services and that I wanted all the sets that had been left with people on incorrect terms back. I gave him a list and said that they had to come back as new and not damaged in any way, and that he would get no commission at all if we didn't get every set back. He reckoned we owed him over £1k in commission. I received all the sets back bar two, so he didn't get any money. Harsh? Maybe, but he had tried to con us. It taught me a lesson about falling for clever sales patter. Did it teach him one, too? I don't think so.

I once advertised for a sales assistant, and got an application from a young lady just out of school. At the interview she was smart and pleasant. No, she couldn't be expected to lug colour sets plus all the test equipment from our delivery vans upstairs to our store room, but she could still make a big contribution. At the end of her first day, I asked her to hoover the showroom carpet – something we all took turns at doing. I then said, 'When you have finished, will you come up to my office to hoover it for me?' She mumbled something about being employed as a shop assistant and not a cleaner. I tried to explain to her that this was something that we all did. She wasn't having it, I could see by the look on her face. I made no comment, and by the end of the week she had gone with a push from me.

I also had difficulties with Stan and his depression. I thought somehow that a better, more responsible job would make it go away, but I underrated how powerful this condition can be. For a long time, he took no time off work and was the bubbly Stan I knew and liked. But he was bottling things up inside. He said one day that his doctor had recommended he have time off work for peace and quiet, where he could recoup. I accepted the situation and he went off sick. I continued to pay his wages and would call in to see him about once a week to see how he was progressing. I was eager for him to return to work, as Lewis and I were covering for him; we didn't mind, as we liked Stan and knew he wasn't shirking, but it was placing a strain on us.

He started back and we carried on; I thought all was OK. Then out of the blue he came into the office one day, saying he wanted to hand his notice in. I tried to persuade him to stay but he had made his mind up; he was going to get completely out of the trade to go and work for his brother selling fruit and veg in one of his shops. (Stan was not a materialistic type of person; as long as he had enough to get by on he was happy, except for one luxury, his touring Bessica Caravan.) We had an argument at this meeting over the amount of his leaving pay and he stormed out of the office. Looking back, I regret this. He and his wife were good people, and he had been a good friend and engineer to me.

If this is beginning to sound negative about staff, I have worked with some great people. When Stan left, I advertised for a replacement. One applicant came down from London for the interview. I was called down from my office to meet him, and found myself facing what could best be described as a hippy, with a long pony tail, scruffy-looking clothes, smoking a pipe with one of those metal type filters as the stem.

Never judge a sausage by its skin, I told myself, and we went up to my office. As we sat down he looked very nervous. I told him to relax, adding, 'We're all just normal people here.' From there on we hit it off. He said he had no qualifications and was self-taught – refreshingly frank. I started talking technical jargon, and he knew his stuff. We discussed the merits of this and that, and if he didn't agree he would say so. I made my mind up straight away – except for one thing: I needed an outside engineer. I explained that our image to our customers was important to us and said, 'If I asked you to cut the pony tail off, would you take the job?' He didn't need to think, answering straight back, Yes. I started him there and then.

I later found out his father was a vicar. He also was better qualified than he said, as he had A level Physics and Maths, had a pyrotechnics licence, and was a qualified first aider. He was also a caving expert, leading rescuing teams when people became trapped. He had no materialistic values at all; his only passion in life was caving. He had been doing it for years and knew the cave system in the Black Mountains like the back of his hand. Before the job with us he would travel down from London every weekend and stay rough at the Caving Club headquarters on top of the mountain at Dan-yr-Ogof.

He spent the first couple of weeks with us on outside calls, but I could see he was better suited to workshop repairs. He and Lewis were getting on fine, so I had a chat with Lewis, and he then became more involved in the workshop. He was a cracker at finding difficult faults. He stayed with us until the business closed, and when it did, I rang a mate and found a new job for him.

Customer service was what we were all about. During my time in business I have not had many altercations with customers. But some people can be impossible…

On one occasion, a man came in wanting to buy a colour television. We discussed prices; he asked for a discount which I said I would give him as this would still leave me my minimal selling price. He kept pursuing more discount, and as it was in the summer and sales were scarce I relented and broke my own rule to offer him a further one. He then produced a newspaper cutting several weeks old with an ad of mine giving a 5% discount with production of this cutting, and asked for it now, on top of the price we had agreed. I said I couldn't give him that as I had just offered him a huge discount. He wasn't having any of that, and said he would take the issue up with the local consumer council.

I replied that I didn't have to sell him the set and, after what he had said just now, I wouldn't at any price, and asked him to leave. True to his word, the following day he came back the following day with a consumer council officer. This was a young man of about 21, who from his behaviour must have been new at the job. The only thing he wanted to know was if I had offered the man the set at the price he said. I did something I almost never do; I told him a porky. The man was furious. I told the young officer that he should use some common sense; if a dealer offers a big discount then someone uses an old advert, he should turn a blind eye.

Another time, a lady of around 25 came in to rent a Panasonic video camera for the weekend. I gave her a lesson on how to use it: I could see she was not mechanically minded so spent more time with her than normal. She seemed happy, left with the camera, brought it back on the Monday saying she had difficulty using it, then left the shop. Later that day, I had a telephone call from someone saying they represented a BBC Radio Wales programme that investigated consumer complaints. She said that her friend was the lady who hired the video camera from me, and asked if I had anything to say, as the programme was going on air the following day. I said it was nothing to do with her and if her friend would come in to the shop I would discuss the matter with her. She went on to say that she would disclose the incident to the public on her programme. I replied, 'So you're blackmailing me then.' She began to say all sorts of things, including threatening to broadcast the name and address of my business. I had had enough of her nonsense, told her she could do what she liked and put the phone down on her. I didn't listen to the programme – I never do – so I don't know what was said. Whatever it was, it had no effect on my business. If the lady who hired the camera had come back to the shop instead of going to the media, I would have offered her a free weekend use of the camera, plus go through again with her how to use it.

You have to keep an eye on other people whose work is essential to the business. I learnt this the hard way, via an incident that could have destroyed us.

I had used the same, highly respected accountants since starting the business. I would visit them once a year, and sit with my accountant, who was also a Justice of the Peace, discussing the financial state of my business. He was always friendly and we got on well together. Then suddenly a tax demand appeared out of the blue for £50,000. I was gobsmacked.

It got worse. The garden that backed onto mine happened to belong to the chief collector of taxes for Swansea, so I went round to politely enquire what it was all about – at which point he said there was also another £50,000 due. He put me in contact with the officer dealing with my case, a very pleasant lady with whom I had a long chat with on the telephone. I asked her to deal with me direct, rather than via my accountant, and not to tell the accountant what was happening. Having established what the picture was, I called the accountant and asked him what was going on. His version of things was nowhere near that of the tax inspectors.

While all this was going on I had to settle the demands, in total £100,000, then try and get some money back. The to-ing and fro-ing between myself, the tax inspector and the accountant went on for some time. In my direct negotiations with the tax inspector, I managed to secure a substantial rebate. One day the accountant came into my showroom and handed me a personal cheque for half this amount. 'It's all been settled now,' he said smugly. 'You can now go on holiday.' I looked him straight in the face and replied, 'That's not my money. It goes back into the business.'

I telephoned a rival accountant in Swansea, Frank Langford, who worked for the buying group I was a member of. I realised he was the man for the job, though his fees were not cheap: you get what you pay for. He agreed to take my account over and pursue the old accountant for the remaining balance. I said that if the old accountant did not co-operate, I would issue a summons and take him to court for recovery. He did not co-operate, of course, so I sent him a letter saying that if he didn't pay up within the next seven days, a summons would be issued against him. In next to no time, I received a cheque for the balance.

Finally, you have to keep your relationships with your suppliers strong. Ours were a delight to deal with.

Panasonic invited me along with another 40 dealers for a two-week trip to Japan, going at the famous cherry blossom time, flying with JAL, known at the time for its first class service. We flew over the North Pole with a refuel at Anchorage, then on to Osaka international Airport. On the flight I could see we were all going to get on together as we had so much in common. Most, like me, had been TV engineers. Many had built up substantial businesses, in some cases with a number of shops.

We were designated a young, charismatic Japanese lad who spoke impeccable American English, who would accompany us for the full fortnight. We were all put up at five-star hotels where we were treated as star guests. Our first day's visit was to Matsushita Electric Company headquarters, owners of Panasonic. We arrived to a fanfare of flag waving from the staff, full of smiling faces. After a meeting with top management, we were shown in detail the large, impeccably clean factory.

What a fantastic eye opener that was. I immediately compared it to the Rank Bush Murphy factory at Earnsettle near Plymouth, which I had visited a while before. That place suddenly looked 50 years behind the times. It had only just acquired one automatic component insertion machine. The staff appeared not to have any pride in their products. The senior engineers were well into their 50s and appeared to lack any innovative ideas. The tuner units used in their sets were well and truly outdated, requiring regular servicing. They had a poor way of pre-checking component reliability. Basically they were living on their past names.

Panasonic, by contrast, had countless component insertion machines. All components were checked to make sure they were up to the standard required; if only one was not, they would send the whole batch back to the manufacturer. We were shown a large bench area, with a screen behind it. On the screen, an operator could see their hands at work, many times magnified, as they controlled delicate cutting instruments carrying out the intricate job of making master circuit boards.

It is said by many that the Japanese are good at inventing. I don't go along with that. The great inventors in early electronic and radio technology were Alexander G Bell (Scottish) for telephones, Guglielmo Marconi (Italian) for radio telegraphy, Harold Hertz (German) for proving the existence of electromagnetic radio waves, and the great American Thomas Edison. More recently, the unsung hero of colour television era is Dr Walter Bruch, a German who invented the PAL (Phase Alternate Line) system. The UK in March 1966 (what a coincidence: the month and year that Pat and I were married) was the first nation to broadcast the PAL system. West Germany followed soon after; PAL is now used by over 100 countries worldwide.

However, the Japanese are brilliant at improving products, innovative manufacture and marketing.

Our journey continued towards Tokyo on the Shinkansen (bullet train), gliding smoothly at speeds of 150 mph as if skating on ice, with views through the windows of people working in the paddy fields, and of Mount Fuji, with its snow-capped volcanic top, a sight to remember forever. We stayed in Hakoni National Park at the foot of the mountain, then on to Tokyo itself, where we stayed for several nights right opposite the Imperial Palace, at the Palace Hotel you could say Japan's flagship hotel. We couldn't leave Tokyo without a visit to Akihabara District, the 'Electric Town', where all the latest electronic innovations were on sale at the cheapest prices you could get anywhere in the world. Many of these items had not yet been exported, and were only on sale in Japan.

We were taken to Mikimoto pearl beds where cultured pearls were grown; back at the hotel there was a shop selling Mikimoto pearls. There was a particular necklace that caught my eye in the window: lovely rounded large pearls all of the same size. They were expensive, but back home they would cost perhaps five times more. I thought about buying them for Pat and let myself be tempted: I knew how chuffed she would be with them.

On one night, we all stayed in a proper Japanese inn called a Rykan. Here you sleep on the floor with a futon style mattress, rolled out, eating real Japanese food like raw eggs for breakfast, sitting on the floor with legs crossed at a very low table, using chopsticks of course, and all kitted out with kimonos. Another Japanese tradition is to take business visitors to a traditional Japanese sauna parlour. You undress into your birthday suit and immerse yourself in a huge shallow pool about a foot deep. Then a group of women appeared clad in white kimonos. They each picked one of us and started to rub us down with a wet flannel. We then went to a large room laid out with flat massaging beds, each with a clean white sheet on the top, where we were asked to lay on our appointed bed, face down. My masseuse started to massage my back, then gently moved down to more sensitive areas... I will leave it there for your imagination. Our hosts seemed very blasé about it all. This was standard practice.

Less intriguing was a theatre trip. We had excellent seats. The actors wore traditional costume and make-up – and everything was in Japanese. I'm afraid we were so tired after our day's sightseeing that we all went to sleep. I felt embarrassed afterwards as I thought the Japanese would take it as an insult, but nothing was said.

Inevitably, when our Japan visit came to the end we said our goodbyes to our Panasonic hosts at Narita Airport and departed on the long flight home, again stopping in Alaska for refuelling, before touching down at Heathrow. I couldn't wait to get home to see Pat and our children.

Soon after, I received an invitation from Mitsubishi, for a three-week tour of Japan and Singapore, this time with my wife. It would take place a year later, also in cherry blossom time.

It was also an amazing experience. We left our children with my mum (who occupied our house for the period, to lessen the disruption to their lives) and flew direct to Singapore. We arrived twenty minutes earlier than expected, but a Mr Peed and his wife's luggage went missing, so we were all held up at the airport, tired after the flight. I tried to lessen the tension by cracking a joke, saying because of the baggage left behind, the jet became lighter and that was why we had reached Singapore earlier. The Japanese burst their sides laughing at this, and texted it to their London office, who also thought it was a great joke, and sent a message back with the same joke (ending that the luggage had turned up in Sydney and would be with us tomorrow). The joke was repeated for the whole of the trip.

Mitsubishi put as all up for the week at Singapore's best hotel, the Shangri-La – a contrast to my previous visit there, where I had stayed in an RAF billet. Mitsubishi took all eighty of us on a night visit to Bugis Street, now a rather staid market, but then well known for its outrageous transsexuals. Everything was done in a humorous spirit. You wouldn't know if someone was male or female; an amazing-looking woman would turn to face you then lift up her skirt to expose large male genitals. We also went to the Botanical Gardens, with their magical display of orchids. The gardens are famous for pressing an orchid leaf with gold leaf and making it into a brooch; Pat was gifted one by Mitsubishi and still has it as a memory of our Singapore trip. Naturally we visited the Mitsubishi factory where all their monochrome televisions were produced at the time. We were the first group of UK dealers to visit this plant, and I'm not sure any other has done so since.

Then on to Japan, where we again stayed at the Palace Hotel, and the dealers visited the production facilities. My main memory is of the company's museum with exhibits shown in date order – there were none from 1941 to 1945. We also followed a similar tourist route to the one I had followed last year, with the addition of a visit to Kyoto – where I managed to get lost. I used to go on training runs, not wishing to lose fitness, but I suddenly I realised I had no idea where I was. All the street names were in Japanese and none of the locals spoke English. My strategy was to keep running, and in the end, I found myself somewhere that I recognised. I was the butt of plenty of jokes after that, deservedly so, given that I was an experienced orienteer (more on this sport later).

It was an amazing trip, but when it ended we felt great to be back home. Caroline and Richard were overjoyed to have their mum and dad with them again. We were back in dreamland; it was very emotional.

CHAPTER FIFTEEN

LETTING THE BUSINESS GO

Eventually, however, the great boom in TVs, video recorders and video cameras began to slow up. Small shops started to go out of business. There was one big dealer in the centre of Swansea, with a superb trading position opposite Swansea market, selling all the top brands including B&O exclusively. A specialist in hi-fi, he had been there for years and years, and I was surprised when he went bankrupt. He had around 100 rental contracts which I bought off the receivers for a song. I recouped my investment within around nine months.

But the market was changing at a deeper level. TVs were now getting reliable and the purchase price was being brought down through overproduction. People were turning to buying their televisions. If my rental customers came into the shop to buy, I would do my best to encourage them to continue renting, but the rental market was now in decline. This was the backbone of my business; in order to keep my rental numbers up I embarked on a mission to buy other rental companies, always buying with my own money, not using the bank. I was successful in this approach.

I opened my second branch shop this way, in Sketty on the outskirts of Swansea, around four miles from us. I think they had around 400 rentals.

They were a retailer like myself, but also had a healthy computer section, which they intended to continue at the same address. The idea was that I would rent the ground floor of the shop, purchasing the retail side and taking all the TV servicing in. The sticking point was the staff of two he had working in the shop; to avoid him paying redundancy money he wanted me to take them as part of the deal. I wasn't keen, but the thought of 400 new rentals, where I would have my investment back in 12 months, was too much of a carrot for me to turn down, so reluctantly I agreed. I had now around 1,200 rentals including video recorders, all serviced from the one place with my existing engineering staff. I was now managing two shops at the same time.

However, this was a short-term fix. My annual charts were starting to show a slow decline, especially rentals, the backbone of the business.

I was also beginning to run out of drive and passion for the business. With new technologies coming in you have to keep pace with it, but I started to let it slide. I started to go missing parts of days in the summer to go cricketing with Richard, or go off and play golf for an afternoon, or go up for half days in the winter onto wild open moorland or deserted forests, searching for new areas to map for orienteering. I loved the remoteness, peace and solitude of these places.

I had built up a good pension fund for myself and Pat through the Equitable Life, at the time known to be the best provider. I calculated that I would retire at 58.

At the same time, retired, well-heeled customers were coming into the shop saying they had never been so well off: their pension pots were converting to massive annuities. They were investing in the stock market, which was now at an all-time high; we were in big bull run and it appeared to be a no-brainer. I would have a set on in the shop showing the Bloomberg Channel with all the latest stock market talk.

I began to plan the best way to offload the business. My children weren't interested in coming in, which I didn't mind, as I wanted them to make their own way in life. By now Caroline had a good degree in her chosen field, and Richard was halfway through his degree in Engineering. There would be no buyers for the business: the big companies wouldn't be interested and nobody small would be able to raise sufficient capital.

I devised a plan whereby some of my staff would take the business over. They would keep the shop – they could have it rent free. I would pay the rates, all the services, water and electricity, plus all insurance. I would keep on all the agencies we had, as without capital they would not be granted an agency. I would sell them the stock at cost price, all profit made on it would be theirs. In return I would keep the rentals; they would service them for me at no charge to me for two years, at the end of which they could take over the rentals for the fee of one year's rental.

Sadly, this did not work out, as the two people in charge, Roger and Simon, couldn't agree on their remuneration. Simon was prepared to cut his wages during the summer low-selling season, while Roger was not. They also decided not to take the option of buying the rentals. Simon threatened to take Roger to court; it dragged on for a while, then they came to an agreement, but the bitterness remained. In the end, I came back to run the shop and they both left.

Pat and I could manage the shop, but what about the engineering? Luckily, I heard that there was a good engineer, Allan, working from a shop in the Hafod area of Swansea as a one-man band. I got hold of him on the telephone, explaining I was looking for someone to do servicing for me. Would he come and see me? We had a meeting at my shop and, after much discussion, came to an agreement that suited us both. I was lucky: Allan was one hell of a nice person; his intellect was far superior to mine and he was an excellent engineer. He just loved fixing things.

The rental market was now in terminal decline, and I had much more difficulty than I anticipated in disposing of the contracts. In the end I sold them to a national company whose main interest lay in money from slot meters – basically they were a credit company. I kept a sale running in the shop, slowly disposing of the stock. The property, which had served me well over almost all of my business life, I put up for sale via a well-known South Wales estate agent, with the instruction he wasn't to advertise it or place a board up but only discuss it with people that had a real interest in it. They kept the property on their books for two years and I never had a single viewing. Finally, I ceased my agreement with them, put my own sales board up and let the word out locally. I had an immediate response from the owner of a wood flooring business two doors down. They wanted to buy the shop, and I agreed a price with them. They then started stringing me along with promises that never happened; in the end I said, 'If you want to buy the property, show commitment by placing a non-refundable deposit of £500 down and I will hold it for you. Otherwise, I'll go elsewhere as I have interested parties wanting to buy.' I promptly received £500 and the shop was soon gone.

I continued the sale right up until the last day I moved out. Allan and I filled a large skip up full of old TV chassis, which over the years we had stripped for spares. Anything left of value I put in store at home in my garage. My desk I used at home as a workbench in my garage, along with a lot of old fashioned wooden storage drawers, which I had bought for £50.00 at an auction when I first started Kendrick Colour. If you're thinking I'm tight, well I prefer to say I'm thrifty. It was engrained in me from my childhood days.

Locking up for the last time I didn't feel sad or elated, just a nondescript feeling. I handed the keys to the new owner, thanked Allan for what he had done for me, especially in staying to the end. I could have sold the Kendrick Colour telephone number to a service organisation, but instead I gave it to him, so my customers would get the service to which they had been accustomed.

Something stuck in my head. A few days before we closed for the last time, we were looking at the Bloomberg channel in the showroom and were chatting about what I was going to do in retirement. I said that one of the things on my list was investing in the stock markets, and he said, 'You've made one fortune; I expect you will go and make another one now.'

I enjoyed retirement. I went training almost every day, running from my house down to our local woods with its steep-sided valley along tracks surrounded by forest, so peaceful and tranquil. There were times on this six-mile run where I would think, 'How lucky I am to be fit and healthy and able to do this.' Then I would think, 'Luck? You make your own luck in life.' And then consider how health problems can hit you out of the blue – then get back to concentrating on my running.

On Sunday morning I would run from my house up into the open moorland around Velindre on a ten-mile circular route and back through the forest, home for a traditional Sunday dinner with Pat and the family. On some days I would go off on my own up into the remote areas of the Brecon Beacons. I'd leave my car parked on some quiet remote road then, armed with a compass and a normal OS map, would jog off into the remote unknown with nothing much other than contours on the map. The quietness, the solitude and the fresh clean air gave me the feeling of floating on air.

Pat and I travelled abroad to see places we had never seen before: Egypt, many of the Caribbean Islands, Cartagena Colombia. We traversed the Panama Canal, sailed up the Canadian Inside Passage, travelled across most of Canada on the Rocky Mountaineer, stayed at Niagara Falls, had a fantastic month travelling the whole of New Zealand in style. And, of course, we visited New York on many occasions when Richard was working there, staying in his posh flat near Wall Street.

I played a lot more golf than before, captaining my club's Quarts team (a team for players with handicaps of 10 or more).

I didn't forget that comment by my engineer Allan when we were watching the Bloomberg channel – but more on the stock market later.

CHAPTER SIXTEEN
ORIENTEERING

Way back when I was running with Newport Harriers, my mates would chat about the new sport of orienteering, a form of cross country running using a map and compass to navigate the course. I didn't get into it then, however.

When I started my own business, the running went to pot as all my time was focused on that. Once I had moved into the shop and employed staff, the pressure slightly came off: on some dark evenings in the winter I would go on short training runs slowly getting my fitness back, and some lunch times I would run from the shop to home, have my lunch, then get Pat to drop me back at the shop. As Kendrick Colour grew and the very good staff I had could manage without me for several hours, I would take a two hour lunch break, take a van home and with a quick change I would go on my favourite six-mile run through the wooded valley, back for a quick shower, eat a quick lunch, then back to the shop, feeling refreshed and ready for action. More than likely a customer was in the shop waiting for me to arrive. This regular training was getting me back to my old fitness levels.

On a Sunday morning I would go on my 10-mile run around Velindre (because of work commitment Saturdays were out). I was able to take

Wednesday afternoons off to race near the BP plant at Llandarcy, over a very hilly road course of around three miles. All the runners were from around the district; we all knew each other and were friends. Every week the race would be a handicap, the fastest runner would be last to start (normally Jim O'Brian of Port Talbot Harriers), the man to start in front of him, if he had been one minute behind Jim last time, would start one minute ahead this time – and so on. In theory that meant that everyone would finish in a dead heat. That never happened of course, but it makes for exciting running as you were always chasing someone. We all loved this; there was great camaraderie and when the race was over we all looked forward to the next one.

One day I saw an ad in the local evening paper with an introductory offer to try orienteering at Singleton Park, Swansea. I turned up. The course, of six lessons over six weeks, was taken by Brian Bullen, the British orienteering champion of that year. I was hooked.

I would go orienteering on Sundays, when the shop was closed. The sport offered me an opportunity to use mind and body. I started attending local club events in the evenings. Running-wise I was far faster than almost all, but on the navigation side, although I was good at reading maps, with an orienteering map I was pretty useless. However, I persevered with it and slowly improved. There were regional league events of a higher standard which I began to compete in.

The first big national event I entered was a run on our patch high up on the mountains in an open, craggy, limestone area up above the South Wales caving headquarters, overlooking Penwyllt near Abercraf. The area was shrouded in mist; you couldn't see where you were going. I was out for hours, more often than not I didn't know where I was, even if I was sometimes only 10 meters from the control flag. I eventually completed the course, which turned out to be some achievement, as a lot of competitors failed to complete.

Aged 44, I won my first Welsh Championships, in 1983. It was at Big Covert in North Wales. I subsequently won eight more times – as you can see if you visit the website of the Welsh Orienteering Association and find their Hall of Fame.

Here's the list. Orienteering is a family sport and operates with age bands, with the older competitors in 5-year age bands, male and female, up to the age of 80. There are short courses for the not so fit. Hence the M (gender) and the numbers (age band) in the list below, with L or S for long or short course. (The first one comes from an earlier time when age bands were different and when courses were called A or B.)

1983	M43A, Big Covert
1984	M45L, Plynlimon
1985	M45L, Ogof Ffynnon Ddu
1999	M60L, Broughton Burrows
2002	M60S, Mynydd Llangatwg
2003	M60S, Pembrey Forest,
2006	M70S, 0gof Ffynnon Ddu
2009	M70S, Wentwood
2010	M70S, Nant Yr Arian

I also once finished third in British Night Championships at M45.

While we are on it, let's not forget Richard, who also features in the hall of fame:

1987	M10A, Brechfa Forrest
1988	M10A, Bryn Alyn

Plus, the British Orienteering Championships, finishing second, in 1987, M10.

I became interested in planning orienteering courses and controlling events. I planned courses for many events and became acknowledged and respected as an expert, planning many prestigious events including the British Night Championships and the Harvesters Relays, the only all-night event on the calendar. There was an annual national planning competition, which I would enter every year. I always finished in the first ten, normally in positions two to six, but unfortunately I never won it. One year, I was asked to be the final judge, which I considered an honour. I enjoyed doing it despite the many hours it took to complete.

I was asked if I would be interested in planning one of the courses for the JK, Britain's largest orienteering event. That year, it was being held around the Aberystwyth area, around 60 miles from my home. It would mean travelling back and forth many, many times, but I didn't mind this as I felt it would be an honour. However, the way I was asked was a disgrace. A Welsh Orienteering Association official in a condescending way asked if I would like to 'apply for the job'. I was already highly respected, so to be treated like that was unacceptable and disrepectful, and I turned it down.

The event turned out to be a disaster. There had been snow the night before. The controller went out, as is the norm, at the crack of dawn to check the course, and as I understand, came back and without consulting anyone cancelled the event. If he had held off cancelling the event, as could have been done by putting everyone's start time back by one hour, all would have been well, for the snow soon cleared. The controller's big mistake was not consulting other senior and experienced officials. He should have come to a consensus opinion. It was just after this incident that the British Orienteering Foundation changed the rules, taking responsibility for cancelling an event away from the controller to the organiser, a backward step I thought. Controllers were carefully selected and graded, with three levels and the top ones being appointed by a knowledgeable committee.

I was asked to control at another JK event, this time near Lydney. I knew the area well, as I had controlled my first major event there, and considered it too dangerous for a big public event, as competitors would have to cross a busy main road on a bank holiday – the JK is held over the Easter period. I told them this, and they never came back to me, though I later found out they had taken my advice and changed the route.

I opened up parts of Wales to orienteering: the bleak areas above Merthyr Tydfil, which stretched for miles right over the top of the Llangynidr Moors past the Chartist Caves and on to the green foothills of Llangattock and Crickhowell.

I carried on orienteering until 2014: my last event and my last Welsh Championships on the sand dunes at Merthyr Mawr. To be honest, I shouldn't have competed, as I was just recovering from shingles and by now (more on this later) I had a heart condition. I entered for the M75, but for some reason there was no short course, so I had no choice: it was the long one for me. My aim was just to complete the course and I just about managed it in two and a half hours. I was more than just exhausted and really struggled in getting back to my car. I then had two days off doing nothing and decided to take a light one-mile jog for recovery. I had covered about half then had to stop. I decided to turn around and go back. I was struggling to make even short steps. I found myself having to get from one lamp post to the next then rest for about two minuets before going on.

When I got back, I said to Pat, 'There's something wrong with me big time.' Apart from my physical state, my mental state was in turmoil, as I thought I was going to die. I knew if I went through the official channels it could take a long time, so I said to Pat, 'Get in the car. I am going to see Consultant Doctor Heatly.' I knew exactly where I would find him, at Singleton Hospital, Swansea.

I asked at the ward desk if I could see him I said, 'Just tell him it's Malcolm Kendrick'. He came out immediately to see me. On the sight of him, tears started to run down my cheeks. I couldn't speak, so left Pat to do the talking. When my emotions cleared a little and I was able to speak, he gave me some paperwork to hand in to have an ECG and other checks.

When these were done, he assessed everything and said he couldn't find anything wrong with me. I looked him straight in the face and replied, 'How do you account for the fact that I could hardly get up the front steps into the building, and when I arrived at the lobby, I had to sit down to rest before proceeding further?'

In the end it turned out I had developed heart failure. From that day on until now I am always gasping for breath, alright sitting in a chair, but even with a slow walk I am gasping. So depressing; it was my own fault; I should not have participated in the Welsh Champs, because I think that's what brought it on.

Naturally, sad to say, that was the end of my orienteering days.

Chapter Seventeen
Dedicated to Aneurin Bevan

I dedicate this chapter to that most famous of all Welshmen, Nye Bevan, who was responsible for the creation of the National Health Service. Without him I would almost certainly not be here now to write this book – I mean no disrespect to the fantastic doctors who with their skills and dedication have helped me to survive and still get something out of life.

One day I went out for a run and after about half a mile I felt a little funny in my head and in general horrible, so I turned around and went back home, saw my GP, who arranged for me to have an appointment in Singleton Hospital for a cardiac check up. I found Dr Weston, the cardiac specialist, to be a very charismatic person, infectious to all around him. I later discovered he was married to a Welsh-speaking lady, who taught him Welsh – I think he must be the only Welsh speaker with a Birmingham accent – and was a terrific trumpet player. He saw me in his little consulting room, complete with a heart scanning machine, and said, 'Life's not fair is it?'

I answered, 'What do you mean?' He replied, 'Here you are, but you've done everything right.' I was still a lean and very fit person.

He diagnosed a septum defect, which I had been told by many a doctor was just a heart murmur. He appeared all excited about this, saying, 'You've made my day.' It was something out of the ordinary. He put me on a treadmill in a room next door; it started slow and then speeded up. I had no problem with the speed, and Dr Watson made a comment to the staff: 'Look at him go! Imagine him with a pair of shorts on!'

He had me in for a coronary angiogram, then continued to monitor me every six months, along with Dr Heatley, who was one of the most honest and caring people I have ever met.

It got to the stage when it was thought I would need stents introduced into my heart. Dr Weston sent me to the stent specialist in Morriston Hospital, Dr Anderson. He discussed my condition with me. I told him I went orienteering, and he said normally he wouldn't look at me but as Dr Weston had sent me, he would. He also said that he had prepared the angiograms in such a way that if I needed stents he could put them in. I don't think he was expecting that I would need stents inserted, but after the operation I had a lousy night's sleep. He came to see me the next morning, finding me in my cubicle slouched over my Daily Telegraph, fast asleep. I woke up and said I was feeling awful. He said, 'I'm not surprised. I had to put three stents in you, one about two inches long.' He added that lucky for me I had 'cross feeding' in my heart. Not much was known about this, but it was the reason I have never had a heart attack, as some blood would be getting to the heart muscle which was about to tear. It was the result of my doing such a lot of running. That put me right for the moment.

But not for long. I carried on orienteering, as before, but was deteriorating rapidly. Dr Weston referred me to Mr Youhana, a specialist heart surgeon at Morriston Hospital. Mr Youhana saw me and put me on his list for a thoracic aortic valve replacement: the aorta had calcified up and was getting narrower as time went on (if I remember correctly it went to less than 1cm, the diameter of a normal pencil head).

I would now go out jogging in the fields and forest, around my home, but I was down to little over one mile. I remember the day before the operation I struggled to get back home; I was gasping for air so much. On the day of the operation when Pat, Caroline and Richard (who had flown back from New York for the operation) came with me to the hospital, I had no fear, thinking I had kept myself fit. I carried my own bag into the hospital. The others looked anxious; I may have looked a little anxious too, but underneath I felt confident that all would be well.

I couldn't have been more wrong.

All gowned up and lying on a trolley, I was wheeled to the door of the operating theatre accompanied by Pat, Caroline and Richard. I tried to cheer them up saying, 'Don't worry, everything will be OK.' I was then wheeled into the theatre, slid onto the operations table, surrounded by Mr Youhana and his team. A mask was put over my mouth and I was out, just like you would switch off a light.

Much of the next part of the narrative I can't remember. I was taken to recover from the op to an intensive care (HDU) ward. Caroline saw I was spitting up blood, but was assured by a member of staff that it was quite normal after this type of op. A number of minutes later I had a cardiac arrest. Apparently all hell broke loose. One of Mr Youhana's assistants was on hand; he opened me up straight away and put his hand around my heart, squeezing it to keep the blood flowing. Lucky for me (looks as if I was born lucky), Mr Youhana was still in the building. He was paged and came walking quickly back, not showing any emotion, but business-like. All this time his assistant had been pumping my heart. Mr Youhana now took control. He decided to operate on me on the bed as it was too risky to move me. He completely opened me up again to repeat the operation – but the repeat operation didn't work. Each time he made the repair, it would tear again.

He was not about to give up. I was on and off bypass all night; apparently the trouble lay in a very difficult place to make repairs, the back of my aorta. Mr Youhana said that my skin was like stitching paper and would just tear. Pat, Caroline and Richard were in the next room all the time, not getting any feedback. At one stage a doctor came out to go to the toilet. Caroline stood in front of the door that he would enter when returning, and wouldn't step aside to let him in. She asked, 'Is everything going to be alright?' He didn't answer her. She said, 'Then I presume it is not going to be alright.' Again he said nothing, and this time she stood aside for him.

A while later someone came out and asked if they had anything to say to Mr Youhana. Caroline piped up, 'Just save him, I don't care what it costs.' (I think at this stage Richard was in denial.) A short while later Julie, the head of cardiac nursing, came out and asked Pat if she wanted to speak to a priest. 'I haven't used one before and I am not going to start now,' was her answer. It would have been my answer, too. Shortly after, someone else came out and told my family, 'If the fire alarm goes off, take no notice. The light above his bed that Mr Youhana was using has just gone up in smoke.'

While all this was going on, I was struggling to survive. I was unconscious but vaguely aware. They had put a tube down my throat, and a nurse seemed to be saying 'Bite!'. It turned out she was saying 'don't bite', but I was biting as hard as I could, trying to send them a message that I was determined and would not give up. I continued doing this for what seemed ages before, for some reason, I stopped.

My acidotic level (the blood's level of acidity) had dropped below a pH of 7, the level taught at medical school at which the operation should stop, and I understand that some members of the team were for this, but not Mr Youhana. In a last-ditch attempt, he wrapped my aorta with Teflon. It worked. Lucky me again. In all, 27 pints of blood were used on me, and all the platelets (a blood clotting substance taken from blood) in the hospital were used up on me.

My family had been in the waiting room all night, not knowing what the outcome would be. Mr Youhana and his team came in looking exhausted, Mr Youhana with his white coat blood-stained and with blood all over his shoes. His knees were in pain as he had been kneeling on them all night. He announced that we were not out of the woods: due to all that had happened, I could well have brain damage, but he wouldn't know yet. Caroline saw that my bed had been stripped down and the sheets were blood red all over. She said to Richard 'Don't look now', and of course that's exactly what he did.

I was sedated in to an induced coma, but I recall my mind was working overtime, trying to get back to the living world. Don't ask me how, I don't know, but I fought like a tiger, exhausting myself to get back from the world of the dead. Apparently, from the monitoring system they knew I was under some sort of stress. I refused to sleep, as I thought that if I slept I would never wake.

This went on for four weeks. I was suffering from sleep deprivation. I had a nurse, Kelly, specially delegated to look after me. I can't remember much about her, but my family said she was brilliant to me. She told me that either Pat, Caroline or Richard were at my bed all the time. A senior night sister with 10 years' experience, she said to me much later, when I returned to visit the ward, that she had never witnessed such brilliant family support before. (She also told me that seeing Mr Youhana at work that night had completely changed her opinion of him.)

In my coma, I had dream after dream. They were all about me surviving. In one dream there was a German heart specialist who used unconventional and illegal methods of trying to save patients, but I didn't care; I would try anything to get back to the living world. In another, I was outside the front of my house at dusk, looking through the large bay window we have into the lounge. I could see Pat, Caroline and Richard discussing me – but they could not see me. I couldn't speak to them, either: in effect I was a ghost. In another ghastly dream, I lay at night in intensive care thinking gorgons were coming to get me. If I looked them in the face, I was dead. They would bob about the room trying to entice me to look at them and it would take all my mental strength not to look them in the eye.

In another dream – or was it a dream? – when I thought I was going to die I called for Mike, a male nurse that I trusted. He came over to me and said, 'What's the matter, butt?' (He was from Neath, and often used the word *butt* in an endearing way.) I said, 'Mike I don't think I can last the night out; look at the instruments; they are saying I won't last.' I asked him to get my son Richard as I wanted to speak to him about my will. He acknowledged what I said then walked away. I asked him again a little while later. I was getting distressed now; again he acknowledged, and walked away. The third time I pleaded with him to get Richard. This time I received a response: Mike said, 'Have you made a will?' I said, 'Yes, yes' – and can't remember anything after that.

In one of the last dreams I remember, Mike was looking after me and said, 'You do know where you are, don't you?' I replied that of course I knew where I was, in a plane over Scotland. He replied I was in Morriston Hospital, and that threw me for I had never heard of Morriston Hospital. The aeroplane I was in had the fuselage completely stripped out with only the inner skin of the outside of the aircraft showing. It was freezing inside and there were beds scattered all around, with patients like me in them, all about to die. There were nurses scattered around the beds, and

Mike appeared to be in charge. In the dream, he was not a nice person and anyone that didn't do exactly as they were told suffered for it. The people around me were slowly dying one by one. The nurses would then strip them of their valuables, to share around themselves. This made me extremely angry, but I was scared to show it, for fear that they could make me the next one to die. I thought, the buggers are not going to get me! Mike would speak to me from time to time, and I would be extra nice to him and butter him up. Then the dawn came up and I felt safe again.

While I was in the induced coma, from time to time Mr Youhana would start to bring me out, but found I was showing signs of distress so would put me back in.

At one time Mr Youhana noticed I was going to catch a cold. This was very bad news, as it could finish me off, so to nip it in the bud I was dosed up with everything conceivable that could prevent it happening. With all these drugs, I was blown up looking like a Michelin Man. Mr Youhana, couldn't understand why I never caught an infection operating in the conditions he did.

Finally, Mr Youhana brought me out of the coma. When he did so, Pat, Caroline and Richard were present. The first person I saw was a nurse looking to see if I was alright. Then I saw my family right behind her. They all had broad, loving smiles. I don't know if I smiled much, but inside I was happy. It was only a few moments, for the nurse said, 'We had better leave him alone now to rest.'

So I am now back in the real world, but still in total confusion. I can remember the large, wide plaster tape covering my insertion wound down the front of my chest, where they had to cut in for the heart operation, being removed. It had all healed up, so I had no discomfort. I can remember being sat up in bed with Mr Youhana on one side and Pat on the other. Mr Youhana was talking to me and I was ignoring him. Pat said, 'Malcolm, don't be rude to Mr Youhana. He is talking to you.' Mr Youhana said, 'Don't worry, it's not important.' I think I was subconsciously blaming him for all that had happened to me during the operation, looking back now – how ungrateful that was of me.

All this time I had been lying in bed, I had lost the use of my limbs. I would get physiotherapy every day to get them working again. I vaguely remember the therapists getting me out of bed and I couldn't stand up. It was difficult for them; I would lie in the bed and they would try to get me to do arm exercises, but I wouldn't. Then Richard would come in and I would do the exercises for him, not them. One physiotherapist went away in tears, as she had failed to do what Richard had done, which showed her dedication to her profession and her patients.

The day before I was moved out of intensive care, Mr Youhana said to Pat, 'Malcolm needs to go into a different environment to interact with other people. He will find it difficult at first but we will keep an eye on him.' The night before I was moved I was taken to a special bathroom where I was placed by a nurse into a seat attached to a hoist, lifted and lowered into a huge bath, then left to splash around and clean myself. The following morning I was taken to the Cyril Evans Ward.

Now I was out of intensive care, Richard was a lot happier. He had been on compassionate leave now for a month. His employer had been very understanding of his family position, especially as at the time he was still only an analyst, so today he flew back to New York.

Cyril Evans Ward, next to the HDU, was where all the patients who have heart surgery recover. Lucky for me, my butty Mike was to keep an eye on me until I settled down. I was placed in a chair by the side of the bed. I tried to get up but couldn't raise myself off the chair; I called over to Mike who was still in the ward. He sorted my problem out by getting me another chair that was higher, which made me chuffed. The next thing before he left I wanted a poo, so he helped me to the toilet and helped me to sit down and waited outside the door. I had to call him for I couldn't wipe my bum and he wiped it for me. I felt ashamed and said to Mike it was a poor show when a grown man cannot wipe himself. Mike never answered; tactful of him.

There were about eight beds in the room, most of the time in the day I would be sleeping. I like my own space with peace and quiet, so I generally kept to myself, not meaning to offend anyone. There was one incident on this ward that stands out: I was lying in bed feeling cold and shivering. I had all my blankets wrapped around me tightly in an attempt to keep warm. I called a nurse over and said to him I was cold; he pulled the bedclothes back and I was in a pool of sweat. He called for help as he could see there was something not right with me. My body began shaking uncontrollably; the nurses were gathered all around the bed and I could see by their body language they didn't have a clue as to what was wrong with me. They put another pillow under me to make me more comfortable...

Luckily, a nurse who was not even a sister came in from the HDU, and in one second she took over complete charge, saying this man is dehydrated. I suddenly thought I was dying. I glanced up at the large clock on the wall to the left of my bed above the entrance to the ward. It was showing exactly 3.45 pm. I thought if I could just hang on a little longer, I would see Pat and Caroline for one last time, as they were due to visit me at 4.00pm. Then Mr. Youhana came in; he had been paged. He was like God, standing at the foot of the bed looking very calm and unflustered, wearing his normal check jacket. He instructed the nurses to draw the curtains around the bed. He looked at me and told the nurses to sit me up then sit me on the side of the bed. I think I then had some water to drink. There was a pause. He was still standing at the foot of the bed and said, 'Sit him in the armchair', which they did. He then walked round to my chair, and got me to stand up to talk to him – at which point I broke down. I caught hold of the arm of his tweed jacket and said, 'I don't want to die' with tears running down my face. I sensed he felt uncomfortable and I felt as if I were begging him. l let go. I still had my pride.

Soon after, Pat and Caroline entered the ward. I glanced up at the clock, which was showing 3.55pm. They sat me down in the chair again. I noticed they left the blood-pressure-recording instrument by my bed and that someone would come in around every 10 minutes to check it. I must have sat in that chair for about two hours not daring to move an inch.

By the next morning, I was back to a stable condition.

I was finally discharged to go home. Pat came to collect me. I was escorted to my car and helped into the passenger seat. I remember saying to Pat after looking at the walnut dashboard, 'This is a nice car.' She said, 'It's yours.'

Driving the four miles home on quiet tree-lined roads on a beautiful sunny day, I felt all the pressures of the past had disappeared. I was on cloud nine. We drove into our driveway; I took one look at the house, then tears came to my eyes. I was so relieved to be home again. Pat helped me with my walking stick into the house, sat me down in my normal armchair. I felt very happy.

I was still in a very delicate physical state. Someone had to be with me all the time. To get up from my chair to go to the toilet was a challenge in itself. First of all I would grab the arm of the chair and pull myself up to a standing position with my walking stick. I would by now have a dizzy head and be gasping for breath. Then it was one pace to the arm of the settee, where I would steady myself and rest for a moment before doing Leg Two of the journey, about three paces to the other arm of the settee. Time to rest again, then the long Leg Three, out of my lounge door to the bottom of our stairs' banister, before the final short leg to the toilet. By that time I was only too glad to have a sit down for a rest before the return trip.

Richard flew back the first weekend for a week's holiday with us. Caroline picked him up from the station. I went to the front door to greet him as he walked down our driveway. I found out later that he was shocked to see the state I was in, a shrivelled up old man, confused, hunched up over a walking stick. Apparently he said to Caroline, 'Why didn't you tell me dad was in such a state?'

However, I was making plans for my recovery. My target was to complete my two-mile warm up run, an out-and-back course down a lane from my house. Unfortunately 'back' was all uphill. I planned to first complete it slowly walking with my stick. I knew this would take a few months. On the first morning I could only get to the corner of my road, around 50 yards away. I sat down on a wall to recover and said to Rich, 'That's enough for today, but I'll be back tomorrow to go a little further.'

As each day went by, I would keep extending it. At the end of the week, when Richard flew back to New York, I had got to 200 yards each way. I rang my golfing mate Eric, a genial, understanding person who had visited me in hospital regularly. He said that when I was ready to tackle the full course I should telephone him and he would come with me. This was another spur to keep me going. As each day went by, I would get closer and closer to my turnaround point. When I had progressed to within about 300 yards of it, I thought, tomorrow it's the whole Monty for me. I gave Eric a bell; true to his word, he came up early the following morning, and we made the walk very slowly with my stick. Now I had someone to chat to, there was never any doubt I would crack it. When I arrived back at the house exhausted, I felt as if I had broken the 4-minute mile.

I continued the exercise daily, leaving my stick in the cloakroom. I started to time myself. My time was slowly getting faster. I never managed to jog the whole course, for I found coming back up the hill too much and I had to walk. I could swear that hill got steeper every time I went up it.

My orienteering club was holding a night event at the far end of the Gower, right on the coast in a flattish sand dune area with forest edging. I thought, that's just right for me. I arranged with my orienteering buddy Dennis, who lived just around the corner from me, for us to go together. My aim was to just complete the course, and I did so – on the slow side, yes, but I felt, as all orienteers do at the finish, stimulated by the event. It's like a drug. I even had a good sweat on, the first time since I had been in hospital. I was now back orienteering, though in future I would have to run the short course and be selective in my events.

I carried on in this way until 2009, when I developed an abdominal aortic aneurism. The operation had been planned at Morriston Hospital, with the intention of stents being inserted. The senior consultant I was under passed the operation to a locum doctor, who was serving his last day at the hospital. Ben, an anaesthetist involved, who was an old school friend of Richard's, said he would keep an eye on me. The night before the operation, this locum doctor came to my bedside for me to sign consent forms. We had a discussion about the operation which left me with the impression that he didn't want to do it. I think we both felt uncomfortable about each other.

I was to be first operation up the following morning. I waited at my bedside, up and ready to go very early. Ben came to see me with the senior lady anaesthetist who would be present. The morning passed and I was still waiting, yet other patients were going in and having operations done. I was wondering what was happening – little did I know, but the anaesthetist and Ben had been batting for me. Purely by chance, the hospital had that day started a consultant specialising in stenting aortic aneurisms. They had never had one before – another one of my strokes of luck.

Eventually, around lunchtime, I was taken up to the operating theatre. When coming out, I was taken and laid on my bed for recovery and rest. The locum doctor came to see me and stood at the bottom of my bed with the senior consultant's assistant next to him. I leaned forward, holding out my hand to shake his, and thanked him for the operation he had just completed on me. He said nothing but accepted my thanks; the assistant gave him a puzzled look, which at the time looked odd but I soon forgot about it. Less than an hour later, a man came hurriedly into the ward straight up to my bed, saying, 'Ydych chi'n siarad Cymrag?' I answered 'Na', meaning no, I don't speak Welsh. He then said, 'I am Chris. I have done the operation on you.'

I thanked him. I think it got back to Chris via the assistant that I thought the locum had completed the op. Chris made a visit to me the following morning to check me ove. I said to him, 'You didn't tell me you were a Mr' (meaning a consultant surgeon). I went on to say he had earned that title and should use it, so when I see him now, I always start the conversation with 'Mr Davies', then revert to Chris. Coincidence would have it that his mother is an enthusiastic orienteer, around my age, and has competed for Wales many times. I had to go back to see him for a check-up a number of weeks later, and as proof to him that I was now back to normal I showed him the winner's 2009 medal for my class I had won at the Welsh orienteering championships only the week before.

I continued orienteering until 2014. Every year I would have an annual abdominal aortic valve check-up under Chris Davies at Morriston Hospital. In 2016, as arranged, I had the check and found I was in big trouble. The aortic valve stent had developed a problem; it had grown in size to 6.5 cm. I was put on an emergency list for the operation. I was now a ticking time bomb. Was I scared? You bet I was. Pat would ring Mr Davies' secretary several times a week; she would leave notes for him but I think he was too busy. Then she rang up one day and mentioned my name to him. Well did he move? Not half, because he remembered I was the first one he operated on in Morriston. It was a weekend; he had me straight in that day, to prepare me for an operation first thing Monday morning. Richard and Emma were on holiday somewhere in Europe; they changed their flights to land at Cardiff to come to see me before the op, arriving just in time, for Mr Davies and the chief anaesthetist were discussing my operation with me as I was about to go in for the op. It meant that all I valued were around me: Pat, Caroline, Richard and Emma. I knew if the op went wrong, they would have a plan B, which I knew was only a 50/50 chance. I said to Chris, 'As far as I'm concerned there's only plan A, and it's going to work like last time. If you have a plan B, I don't want to know about it because we won't need it.' I asked Chris what his batting order was; he paused then said, 'You're batting and I am bowling.' Little did I know I was the only op of the day. My family came to the door of the operating theatre with me. I had probably been sedated by then; I said my goodbyes with my mind accepting that this could be the last time I would ever see them. The theatre door closed behind me.

The theatre was packed full of medical people, with about four consultant anaesthetists around me. Mike the pacemaker specialist was there. I lay there looking at the ceiling, thinking this may be the last time I closed my eyes. The chief anaesthetist put the mask over my mouth – then I knew no more until coming around in a post operation unit with a specialist nurse looking after me, encouraging me and making me feel good. She didn't need to; I was elated. I was kept there for about an hour, before being taken back to my ward for recovery and my family to see me once more. It looked as if my luck had held out again: thank you Mr Davies and your team.

I haven't mentioned it before; I collapsed and momentarily passed out on a walk. I managed to get home; Pat called my local GP and he immediately summoned an ambulance to my home. I was then taken to A&E, kept in to have a pacemaker fitted, by Dr Barry. This was a saga in itself as Mr Purnell, the consultant dealing with me, said that after doing tests he couldn't find anything wrong with me but would make one more check before discharging me. I thought there's no way I am leaving this hospital as there's obviously something wrong with me. The following morning I was taken for a treadmill test. I waited with the treadmill technician; I said to him, 'Normally I have no fear of going on a treadmill, but this time I have, because I will black out.' Mr Purnell arrived to carry out the test; I started on the treadmill with a blood-pressure-reading gadget around my left arm. The treadmill started to move, very slowly, then almost immediately Mr Purnell stopped the proceedings. 'We are keeping you in to have pacemaker fitted,' he said.

I said to him, 'I am so glad, not that I want a pacemaker fitted, but that you have diagnosed the problem.' Looks like I dodged another bullet. I thought this was a wise decision of Mr Purnell to have Doctor Barry fit the pacemaker, for he has specialist skills in heart rhythms. Dr Barry said, 'I am going to recommend you have an internal cardiac defibrillator (ICD) fitted.' After the meeting I waited and was called by the hospital to have this done, and that's as it is today. I'm glad to say it's never fired off.

At another time, I got pain in my back and was diagnosed as requiring a hip replacement. I decided to fish Richard's old bike out from my garage, dust it down, then try it out as an exercise. It worked: sitting on the bike and pedalling there was no pain. There were more than twenty gears, so I would have no problem with the Welsh hills that surrounded me. I would travel in the lanes and over the hills for up to twenty miles, every other day if I could. However, as time went by I would have to change down in gears, until eventually I was down to the lowest gear and the strength in my legs was hardly sufficient to move the pedals.

I decided to buy an electric bike, one of the best health investments I ever made. I now ride it on alternate days, cycling up to 20 kilometres along the leafy lanes and mountain moorland around my home. It gives me enormous health benefits. Mentally it both relaxes me and sharpens my concentration, keeping an eye out for potholes, of which there are many. I suppose you could say these are two opposites, but that's as I see it. My reaction time is kept at its best, along with my sense of balance. My heart circulatory system with all the devices implanted, is given a good workout – around 40 minutes, they say, is about the length to feel benefits. My muscles get to have a good exercise. When I finish, I feel refreshed all round, if not a little tired.

When I ride, I wear a Phillips medical type GPS watch around my wrist, which monitors my heartbeat, speed and altitude, and maps the course I cover. I download this onto my computer to view everything that's happened on my ride, and to compare with past performances also stored there.

You may think, why do all this, given your health problems? Why don't you be like a normal person, just walk around with your stick and use an invalid buggy? Well, is there such a thing as a normal person? Doctors advise me that I'm doing the right thing for longevity.

Mind I do have my problems on the bike. I have a constant fear of falling off, which I have done on a number of occasions, after which I find it difficult to get up and remount. One recent example occurred when going over a humpback bridge. Just about to get to the brow, I inadvertently switched my electrics off, leaving insufficient strength in my legs to power the bike. I came to an immediate standstill, and fell over on my left side. As I went down (still on the bike), I instinctively turned my shoulder to break the fall. Though I was, of course, wearing a cycling helmet, I felt a crack as the back of the helmet hit the roadway and a huge pain in the back of my neck. My immediate instinct was to get up, but I found I couldn't. In addition to my head, I had done something to my left leg.

Luck came to my aid again. I was now lying on a public road, unable to move and, due to the bridge, invisible to traffic coming in the opposite direction. But the driver of the car behind me stopped, leapt out and ran up to the crest of the bridge to stop oncoming traffic. Even luckier, she turned out to be a nurse, and insisted I go straight to hospital. Pat and Caroline were notified, and within ten minutes they were with me. I was taken to A&E, and as I was on Warfarin, I was attended to quickly. They kept me until around 2am, giving me the full Monty: head scan, leg X-ray, ECG. Lucky for me the neck injuries were not serious, and my ICD had not fired off.

I know; I can't keep dodging bullets like this. One will hit me one day, but it's better to go like that, than to be a crumpled up old wreck with no brain sitting in an armchair.

Chapter Eighteen

A Novice Investor

I would like to start this part of the book by giving a well earned tribute to Warren Buffet, acknowledged as the best living investor. I shall quote his rules of investing. Rule One is 'Never lose money' and Rule Two is 'Don't forget the first rule'. Benjamin Graham, considered the best investor of all time, is cited by Mr Buffett as saying 'Investing is most intelligent when it is most business-like'. Buffet goes on to say that these are the nine most important words ever written about investment. I can't argue with that. However, I get vibes from Graham's work that he has a tendency to look forward (i.e. into the unknown) as opposed to looking back, at facts. The method that I would go on to develop would follow the second option (looking back) and avoid the dangers of the first.

To cap both of these giants of investing, pride of place for me goes to Dow and Jones. Their work is particularly impressive as all they started their work with was a scribbling pad, and because they showed unshakable honesty and integrity, and were never bought by anyone. I shall say more about them later – but now, back to the start of my investment career…

On my retirement the stock market was on a big bull run. Many people I knew, like retired customers who visited my shop, commented on how fantastically well they were doing in the stock market. It looked as if you couldn't go wrong.

I had built up a good pension fund for both myself and my wife. I had sold my villa in Spain. When I sold the business I had cash from that. It was no good leaving it in the bank, so I heeded the advice from those around me and decided to invest it. I contacted a company based in Bristol which had had a good write up in the Daily Telegraph. An advisor came to see me who specialised in pensions. His name was Jon Briggs, and he was the first and best adviser I ever met. Almost all the rest have just been hard-nosed, looking to take you for all you're worth and possessing little in-depth knowledge of how shares' and stock market funds' performance actually relate to risk. Jon talked me through where I should place my investments to see Pat and myself through our old age. I liked what I heard.

I had also had discussions with my bank, but didn't like their offer or their style of investing: the funds were all UK-based and the advisors, though very pleasant to deal with, didn't seem to have really deep knowledge.

I visited a financial adviser in Cardiff, who had had tremendous write ups in the national newspapers. She sent me a breakdown of what she would do and of what she would charge. I turned it down and she rang me up to find out why. I said her charges were too high, and she instantly halved them. I asked her why, and she said it was because she liked me.

I went to meet an advisor from a big City firm. They showered me with facts and graphs. All my money would go in funds of their own, and whether those went up or down, they would take their management fees. There was no incentive for them to do well by me. After the meeting, they kept telephoning me at home.

I stayed with Jon.

We did well until Lehman Brothers collapsed in 2008. Jon had put me into a number of zero dividend preference shares. At the time these were considered the best thing since sliced bread, but after the collapse, some of these were wiped out. My portfolio halved in value.

How much further would it fall? The system seemed in a state of collapse. I had lost half my life savings in a few months.

All experts in finance say, 'Don't sell. Over time the value will come back.' I thought, 'They are the experts. I would be foolish not to take their advice.' Luckily I didn't need the money then, but there were others I knew who had bought at the top and were now selling out at the bottom.

Of course the experts were right in the long term, but I found myself wondering how much money they made out of me. I had bought some funds with a 5%, upfront fee, plus fund management charges of on average 1.5% a year, plus commission on deals. The answer seemed to be that they had been making a lot of money out of me, with me taking all the risk. A nice little earner if you can get it.

'OK, big boys,' I thought. 'I will change all this.'

I had already brought some ISAs through a discount broker (discount brokers don't offer advice or recommendations, just carry out transactions for you and handle the paperwork at a reduced fee). This broker also turned out to have an excellent 'platform' (I shall say more on this later), and I have continued to trade through.

I started reading books on investing.

I began buying and selling shares. I tried day trading, short-term holding and long-term holding. I did not go into CFD (Contracts for Difference, effectively betting on indexes) as I couldn't understand it.

It wasn't an easy ride. I made some good calls, but also mistakes, some of them costly – an investment in Enron, for example.

I came to the conclusion that investing in individual shares was too risky, and now only invest in funds.

As I invested, I found 'technical analysis', the basing of investment decisions on a close study of charts showing the past performances of indexes and of individual investments, more and more interesting. My reading became more specialised, zeroing in on this topic. I have made a reading list at the back of this book, but the two books that I learnt the most from were by John J Murphy. They are *Technical Analysis of the Financial Markets* and *Charting Made Easy*.

I also learnt more about the man responsible for 'charting'. Charles Henry Dow was born in 1851 in Connecticut, USA. He was poorly educated and, interestingly I thought, rumoured to be dyslexic. Through sheer persistence he managed to get a job with the Providence Journal, the only continuously published daily newspaper in the USA at that time. He was given the job of writing business stories. He researched these with great care. His editor, Danielson, became so impressed with this, that he assigned Dow to accompany a group of investors and businessmen on a visit to the mining boomtowns of Colorado, where the young reporter experienced capitalism in its rawest form and wrote about it in his 'Leadville Letters' (in which he coined what is now an investment cliché, that the mines he found there were not places 'for widows or orphans' to put their money).

With a rising reputation as a journalist, Dow moved to New York. He soon invited a fellow reporter from the Providence Journal to join him. Edward Davis Jones, of Welsh ancestry, had shared both Dow's fascination with business and his dislike of the dodgy practices of the time, whereby financial reporters were regularly bribed, by individuals promoting a stock, to write favourably about that stock.

Dow and Jones started their own agency in 1882 (with a third journalist they had met in New York, Charles Bergstresser). Their trade was providing quick, accurate updates of company and market information. Next year, they published a daily newsletter, which also included two indexes they had created to measure overall market performance. In 1889, they produced a fully-fledged newspaper, the Wall Street Journal. This was aimed at being a paper of news but not of opinions, crusading for honesty in reporting.

Dow also developed the first chart theory of investment analysis. The essence of his approach was to isolate lasting 'primary' trends in market movements, distinguishing these from 'secondary' or even 'tertiary' short-term ups and downs. Secondary or tertiary moves can be brief corrections, reactions to one-off bits of news or the result of manipulation by dodgy market participants.

In essence, he looked at his two indexes, which were for transport stocks and industrial stocks. If both were heading up, the market was in a genuine, lasting, 'primary' upward trend, which should last at least a year. If the two indexes began to differ, that would be the time to become cautious. When they were both falling, the market was falling. Time to sell. When they differed again, the market was reconsidering and it could be an excellent time to buy. (This is an oversimplification, as he also used other criteria, such as volume of business, to establish the quality of trends.)

Dow never published a formal book on his theory, but talked about it in editorials in the Journal. His theory was later developed by other thinkers, notably William Hamilton, who wrote further pieces on it in the Wall Street Journal after Dow's death in 1902, and Robert Rhea, who wrote it up in a book (and did Dow the honour of calling his book *The Dow Theory*) in 1932.

While studying charts in depth, I kept attending seminars on investment. I was not impressed by these.

A London-based wealth management company was advertising a free event at a swanky hotel around 40 miles from Swansea, with a free nosh offered. Pat and I booked up. We went with an open mind, or half-open, anyway. I had done a little research on this company; the reports were very enlightening, but sad to say not very good.

There were about 35 people, most of around pensionable age, present for the talk which would last two hours with a break in between. I found the talk very professionally presented, interesting and informative, but decided before the end of the meeting it was not for me. I was amazed at the number of well-educated, intelligent professional people who seemed sold by it all and agreed to put their life savings with someone they had known nothing about a few hours back. Now that's what I call brilliant salesmanship – though to be fair, they didn't oversell to me. One of their salesmen engaged me in a conversation. I told him about the way of investing that I was developing, and he asked me about the taxation issues that my approach raised. I replied that I was aware of these, to which he said, 'We can't help everybody and you're one of those people.'

I received an invitation via the internet for a free course on investing. By now, I would normally ignore such a thing, but this particular course said it would cover Dow Theory along with other investment approaches. That was music to my ears (let's forget I am almost deaf for a moment). I said to Pat, 'I am going to that course.'

She said I couldn't because of my health – but with family assistance, we managed to make it all possible. There were about 40 attending the meeting. Talking to some before it, I said I had come to learn about Dow Theory. They had heard the word Dow but seemed absolutely clueless about anything else connected with him.

The company, which turned out to specialise in spread betting, wanted you to put money into an account before the meeting. I said, 'I don't know anything about you; would you put a six-figure sum into something you know nothing about? Think about it.'

The presentation, which apparently they conducted on a regular basis, was as usual very well done. The person giving the talk was well respected in the City. Richard came with me and sat quietly taking it all in; I was the one with the big mouth doing the talking. The presenter was showing us charts saying when to buy and not to buy. On one chart, I think it covered a 3-year period with a steadily escalating price, and he chose a period in the middle saying it was a good time to buy. This part of the chart was virtually flat, so I piped up that I wouldn't buy there as it was showing no buy signal, and that hindsight was a wonderful thing. He was not impressed.

He spent a good time talking about placing stop losses (I talk about these in the next chapter), which everyone seemed interested in except me. I asked him if he had a systemic way of working out where one should put the stop loss, and after some discussion he admitted it was just a guess based on his past knowledge. I asked him questions on Dow Theory, to which he didn't have answers. Instead, he asked me if they were trick questions, to which I replied, no, they weren't and that I'd been hoping they might be able to answer them.

During my research for this book I thought it would be a good idea to read some other books that have been written on investing in the financial markets. A couple came especially recommended, but I was not impressed by either.

One was written by a UK financial advisor and had plenty of sensible information, but only skirted around the best ways of making money in the financial markets.

Financial advisers tend not to be great stock-pickers, as that is a very specialist area. As a result, they often put investors into funds, and this means two sets of fees: theirs and the fund managers. These disappear before you get any return from the investments, and the risk is all yours.

I got the sense that this was a good book for the author to hand out to clients to raise his profile, but not the mine of information I was led to believe it would be.

The second book, was written by an American fund manager well known on Wall Street for his undoubted success and relentless dedication to his profession – so much so that it affected his home life, as he was unable to be with his children as often as he would like. To me, this is taking the pursuit of wealth too far. In the end, what's the money for?

He is clearly a very smart man, but the book left me very confused, about himself and his methods of trading. The author admits to frequent trading in and out of the market, yet in other places encourages the holding of stocks for the long haul. He admits to having a big ego. I do not think this is the best thing for a trader, who should be cool and a calculating thinker. He is obviously a high risk taker, getting a buzz from it all, getting his daily fix as it were. He actually says remarkably little about lessening risk, probably the most important thing about investing in my view.

Perhaps the most interesting part of the book was a quote which he had as a one-liner in bold type.

'You can't see the future though the rear-view mirror'

I had come to the conclusion that this was totally wrong. Dow Theory looks at the facts, past history. It doesn't engage in crystal ball gazing into the unknown future.

In the author's defence, he has proven to be a brilliant stock picker. Would I buy into his fund, with his past record? You bet I would, but in a balanced way alongside other funds. Any downturn and I'd head straight for the revolving door.

All in all, there seems to be a lot of uninspiring advice out there. Luckily for me, I didn't use any of it to risk my own money. Instead, I had developed my own approach, which I shall describe in the next chapter.

CHAPTER NINETEEN

MY METHOD

After around twenty year of investing I had moved on from the novice stage, and created my own method of trading.

A question that you have to ask yourself as you read about it is, 'Would I do this well?' A trading method has to suit your personality: the way you think, the way you react. Are you cool or do you panic under stress? Have you got patience? As well as understanding the market, you have to understand yourself.

My method is 90% about reading charts skilfully: the more competent you become at this, the more success you will have. Rather than give a tutorial here, which would inevitably be superficial, please read the classic texts on the subject, which I have already mentioned: John J Murphy's *Technical Analysis of the Financial Markets* and *Charting Made Easy*. Read these before you do any investing, and keep studying them once you begin to invest. The best traders have them on their desks and regularly refer to them, learning more all the time about the craft of understanding what the market is saying about itself through charts. You never stop learning.

You must choose a broker with a good online 'platform'. The best ones provide detailed charts of the historical performance of market indexes and of individual investment vehicles – stocks and shares, but also bonds and funds (the one that I use documents over 2,500 funds). The charts must cover a wide range of timespans, from 10 years to 2 days. The longer timespans may seem ancient history, but they are essential.

A good platform also allows you to overlay several charts, so you can compare performances and indexes.

In the material below I refer to the 'sell button'. A good dealing platform has one of these which, if you press it, doesn't actually make the sale but tells you how much stock you can sell. This information, as I shall show later, can be very useful. If you have the stock, you then have to press another button, 'Confirm', to actually make the sale.

Having studied the two classic books and found a good broker, it is time to start investing.

I have certain rules, which you must abide by to make my method work well:

Rule one   **Protect your assets**
Rule two   **Don't forget rule one!**
Rule three   **Buy into an ascending graph**
Rule four   **Buy into funds not shares**
Rule five   **Hold a number of funds**
Rule six   **Keep it in ISAs or SIPPs** (UK residents only).

Let's take **rule one,** protect your assets. I am amazed that I cannot find more on the importance of this by googling on the internet. The nearest that I can find is Warren Buffett's 'Don't lose money'. Buffett has broken his own rule many times in the past, however. Anyone who invests has lost money at some point, so there's no disgrace in that. (On the subject of Warren Buffett, I don't feel that smaller investors should follow his investment strategy and buy everything he buys. He buys for complex reasons, including synergies between companies.)

Remember, you can always take your money out of an investment and hold it in safe cash until you see an opportunity to go back in again at a lower price.

Rule two, don't forget rule one!

Rule three, buy into an ascending graph. The price of an investment can start to fall, at which point 'fans' of that investment think it is a good time to pick up stock cheap. But this is looking forward, not listening to the chart. Wait until the price starts heading in the right direction – up – before buying. As the old investors' motto has it, 'Never try and catch a falling knife.'

Rule four, buy funds not shares. Funds contain a large number of shares, thus creating balance and stability. Individual shares are a high risk. If a hedge fund attacks a share – in other words a company – it can destroy it. Other, often random factors can affect a share price drastically, too.

Rule five, hold a number of funds. Having all your eggs in one basket – even if it is a fund – is risky. I consider that the ideal number of units to hold is about ten, as this gives you a better spread of the whole market – don't forget that your investments can cover the globe, not just the UK. If you have a relatively small amount to invest, five funds should create a good spread of risk.

Your investments must be well researched, by which I don't mean per earnings ratios, profit warnings or any accountancy side of the fund, but what the fund's chart shows you of its historical performance. (The technicalities of each company within the fund I leave to the discretion of the fund manager.)

Given the huge number of funds out there, there is no substitute for taking time over this research. Look at lots and lots of charts. Keep your eyes and ears open for recommendations, but *always* check these against the charts, and if the charts don't look brilliant, don't invest, however wonderful some expert says a fund is.

As well as past performance, look out for volatility, which is the degree to which the investment's value varies over time. Ones that roar up and plummet down are 'highly volatile'. I am not a lover of high volatility and usually look for low volatility and steady growth.

In my case I almost never buy a fund if it has a 'spread', that is a difference between the buying and selling price. Some funds have ones as big as 1%. For the 'buy and hold' investor, this does not matter that much – though it's still another way that money finds its way from the investor's pocket into that of the financial institution. But for the trader, who buys and sells frequently, this is bad news.

I might break this rule if a fund seems really good and the spread is quite small. But there are funds out there with no spread at all: the sale price and the buying price are the same. I prefer to trade in these.

I also look at the ongoing charges of the fund.

Finally, consider the investment philosophy of the fund manager. This should be mentioned in the fund prospectus or on their website. How much risk do they like to take? Only invest in a fund if you are happy with their attitude to risk at the time at which you are investing.

Once you have chosen your funds and bought into them (more on this later), keep your eye firmly on them. Have a daily glance – once a week is not enough – and check how each one is performing. You need to have a benchmark for their performance. I keep it simple and use the FTSE 100 and 250. Alternatives are the Russell 2000 (for smaller companies) and the S&P 500 in America.

If a fund is performing poorly, look for another with better performance, and swap. Don't get attached to a fund; have no scruples; dump it as the fund manager would dump a stock.

Rule six, keep it in ISAs or SIPPs. This way, everything is kept in a 'wrapper' free of any tax. If you cash in an investment, do not take the proceeds out of the tax wrapper. They can be left there, in cash, until such time you use them. Once the money is out of the wrapper, the tax man will be looking for his share.

Managing risk is almost as important as buying the right funds. The first thing that financial advisors ask you is, 'What is your attitude to risk?' They then construct a portfolio in the light of your reply. They are legally bound to do this – but for the serious 'technical' investor, this is not really a meaningful question. Your attitude to risk should vary according to what the charts are telling you. If a fund looks to be in a serious uptrend, then I would take on risk and buy. If the fund is falling, I would become very risk-averse.

On a broader level, if the market is looking healthy overall, I would be tempted to consider more volatile funds. I've already said that I am naturally cautious and avoid highly volatile investments. But if I am convinced that the market is set to rise, then I would be a bit more adventurous. If the market is falling, I would look to be in a cash or a money market fund (more on this later).

My response to any financial advisor's question about risk would be that my attitude changes day by day, depending on the charts. That's probably not what they want to hear.

I do not involve myself in 'shorting' stock – selling investments that I don't possess, in the hope that I will be able to buy them back later. Hedge funds do a lot of this, and do well out of it, but it is too risky a game for the private investor. Only trade funds that you hold in your portfolio.

Incidentally, I avoid one method of (in theory) taking risk out of trading, the 'stop loss'. This is a way of, in theory, covering your investment by telling the broker to sell at a particular point if an investment goes the wrong way. So, for example, if you buy something for 250p, you can put in a stop loss at 240p, which means that if the stock price starts falling, the broker will sell at that price. If the price keeps on falling, say to 150p, all you have lost is 10p, not £1. Sounds magical!

However, I question whether that works in current markets. Stop-losses can be 'spiked out'. There are some unsavoury people out there who will drive prices down to trigger stop-loss sales, pick stock up cheap that way, then watch the price move up again. I learnt the hard way; when I began investing, I used stop losses, and found these being set off by spikes. Am I cynical? You bet I am.

A quiet, insidious risk faced by the private investor is the one caused by the long settlement periods on many purchases. In my opinion, this is the worst enemy of the individual-in-the-street investor like myself. It means that there is a long time – it can be 5 working days – between making a purchase (and parting with your money) and the investment vehicle you have bought actually being yours. If the investment should suddenly take a dive during this time, you cannot exit and will take a big loss. By contrast, large institutions – who have the use of your money over this time – can move instantly, however and whenever they want.

Even if your money is in a client account, held on trust, the institution can make money from it.

The financial playing field favours large institutions over the private investor; it is my opinion that the regulatory authorities should consider appointing a panel of independents to address this anomaly.

I have devised a way of reducing this risk. Buy slowly. Once you have identified a fund and once the charts are telling you that the market is right, dip a toe in the water. Make a small investment, say £500. Monitor it for five working days, checking via the 'sell' button to find out when the stock is 'clear'. Once it is clear (in other words, once you are free to sell it all at any time of your choosing), then buy another £500. When this is clear, you can invest £1,000, safe in the knowledge that if the market turns unexpectedly, you can get half your holding out straight away. Build your holding over time.

I call this risk-avoidance technique the Kendrick Method. Let's see if it catches on, then I will be remembered for something!

The alternative is risky. Markets can be volatile. If you invest £10,000 straight off, and the market has a sudden attack of the jitters, it can fall 5% while you are waiting for your stock to clear (there were three quick 5% falls in 2018, and in other years these quick falls have been further). Result, you have lost £500, and you have the painful experience of seeing your investment shrink and not being able to do anything about it.

To end this section, I'd like to say something about the danger of greed. You have to be disciplined in investing, and do what the charts tell you. But in reading charts there is always room for interpretation, which means that there is always room for excessive optimism. When you become unsure, when you start thinking 'it's 50/50 whether the chart is positive or not', then you should seriously consider selling.

If this happens soon after an investment has been made, then take your profit, even if it's small. It's better than a big loss. Like weather, markets can change quickly. Be content with what you've got.

So here are four more rules:

Rule seven   No 'shorting'
Rule eight   No stop loss
Rule nine   Be aware of lock-in (Use the Kendrick Method)
Rule ten   Don't be greedy. Be prepared to take a small gain.

I want to say a little about investing in uncertain markets. Make sure you are holding bonds as well as funds.

Let's say you want to invest £100,000. As suggested, spread this evenly across 5 investments, 20% in each. As well as low-volatility, 'defensive' (safe) funds, you could invest one portion in a money market fund and another in a sterling high yield bond (look for extremely low volatility).

As usual, wait for the market to tell you it is time to buy. Wait for two 'upticks' (days on which your chosen investment has gone up in value), then buy in slowly. I would follow the pattern below...

20%	20%	20%	20%	20%	of your £100,000
1	2	3	4	5	Number of holding
F	B	F	B	F	Buy one per day, in this order

(F = Fund, B=Bond)

When buying bonds, you can jump in and buy larger amounts. They clear more quickly than funds, and their prices tend to move much more slowly so are very unlikely to fall with the speed that shares or equity funds can.

If a bond turns out not to perform, do some more research. Check the weak bond's performance against other bonds using the overlay feature of your broker's platform. Some bonds move in opposite directions to one another. Consider switching to one of these.

Should you be fully invested at all times?

Most financial advisors and investment houses will say to you that your investment money is best when fully invested. They are right up to a point, for when your cash is waiting on the side, it's not going up in value. However, it's not going down in value either. Why leave it invested when the markets are going down? Are you going to stand by daily and watch them keep dropping? I won't. We are back to rules one and two again: take your money off the table and wait to go in at a lower price, when the fund has started to turn up again. You'll get more shares for less money. When you do start reinvesting, don't forget the Kendrick Method: build your holding slowly.

Albert Einstein and compound interest

Investment houses consistently make a big fuss about the power of compound interest when discouraging trading and, instead, promote a 'buy and hold' strategy. They often quote Albert Einstein, who is reputed to have said it was 'the eighth wonder of the world' and to have added, 'He who understands it earns it; he who doesn't, pays it.' They don't usually add that the great physicist lost most of his money in the 1929 crash.

The principle says that if you reinvest the interest paid on a sum of money, that sum will get exponentially bigger. The 'rule of 72' says how much bigger – you will double your money in x years, where x is 72 divided by the rate of interest. So at 6%, you'll double your stake in 72/6 = 12 years (and quadruple it in 24 years).

However the principle has flaws. Let's say we invest £1,000. If you have to do so via a managed fund, there will be some sort of charge to start with. This can be up to 5%. If you go through a financial advisor, he will want his cut, too, which could be another £50. So at the end of the first year you will have invested £1,000 less the deductions, leaving you with £900. Add the 6% growth (if you're lucky) and that is £954. You'll only show any profit three quarters of the way through your second year of holding the investment. Of course, you would also have to pay an exit fee on realizing the gain (when you eventually get it).

Yes, in 12 years you would have doubled your £954. But people can't always sit on money for that long a time. Many things can crop up, such as a sudden desperate operation on a loved one. Or the underlying market could fall, which can erode the investment further. It is hard to stand back and watch your investments disappear by the day in the hope that one day they will return. It takes a braver person than me to do that; I've done it and stuck it out, and won't be doing it again.

Compound interest is not the magic bullet its advocates make it out to be.

If I think the market is in for a major fall, I de-risk my portfolio even further by holding more cash.

Remember that when you are fully invested, your fund managers continue to take their cut. Whether your portfolio is up or down they make as much as or more than you. That is why you should, if you can, take control of your own investments.

Although not relevant to my method of trading, I should touch on investing in individual stocks and shares. The constant buying and selling of these creates huge profits for the market operators and associates.

While such activity can create huge gains within a short time, it can also cause huge losses. In addition, the government makes things worse by slapping a 0.5% tax on any trade in shares. It is said that around 10% of private, individual investors make money on dealing in stocks. Hence my rule four above.

Using my principles, I look for annual returns of 20% to 25% plus dividends and with no income tax to pay – but I must conclude by saying that I can't accept any legal responsibility for any advice given here. I have written this part of the book because I genuinely want the wealth created in this country to benefit the person in the street not just financial experts – but I can't guarantee that everything here will work for you. A lot of it is about getting a 'feel' for charts and what they are telling you, and there is no substitute for study and experience in acquiring that. Nobody writing about investment can guarantee an outcome. If they say they can, beware!

Chapter Twenty
Using Charts

I'm not going to provide a full tutorial on this – the authors I have mentioned do a much better job of this than I ever could. However, I would like to show some charts and make a few comments, which I hope will give you a flavour of this way of investing, which has done well for me.

The charts that I present show:

- A fund that I am tracking (in red)
- The FT100 (dark blue)
- A money market fund (brown: by far the least volatile of the lines)
- Two other funds, for comparison (purple and light blue).

I'm not going to name names, but the funds are all ones that I have researched and followed, so are quality ones.

The first chart shows the performance of the investments over two and a half years. This is the kind of timespan I would look at to make my initial selection of a fund to invest in, though I'd look at lots of different timespans before I finally decided.

Try taking a piece of paper, holding it over the chart and slowly moving it across the page left to right. Ask yourself 'would I buy now?'

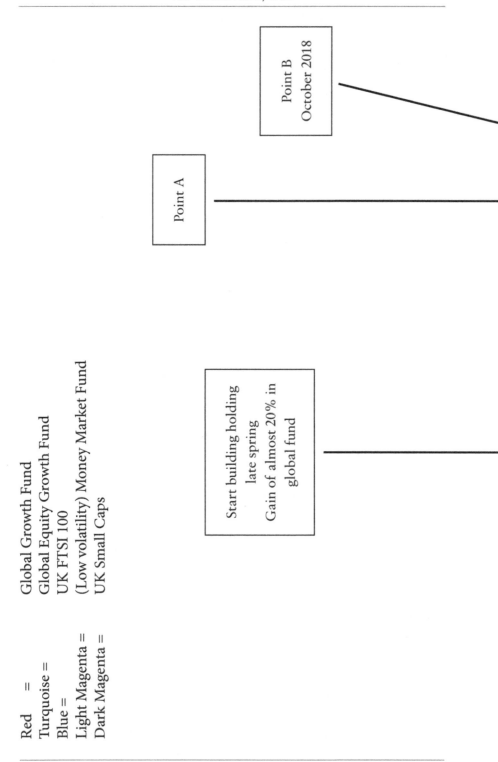

Red   =   Global Growth Fund
Turquoise =   Global Equity Growth Fund
Blue =   UK FTSI 100
Light Magenta =   (Low volatility) Money Market Fund
Dark Magenta =   UK Small Caps

Point B
October 2018

Point A

Start building holding
late spring
Gain of almost 20% in
global fund

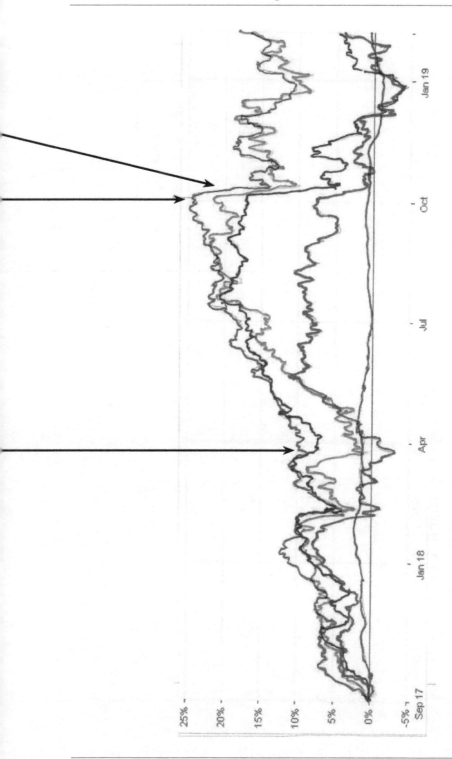

Chart A: three year chart (built on data from the LSE)

Red = Global Growth Fund
Turquoise = Global Equity Growth Fund
Blue = UK FTSI 100
Light Magenta = (Low volatility) Money Market Fund
Dark Magenta = UK Small Caps

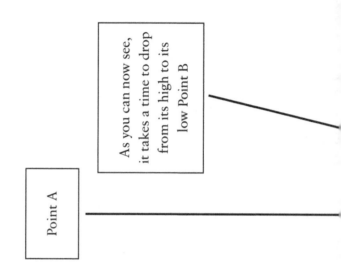

Point A

As you can now see, it takes a time to drop from its high to its low Point B

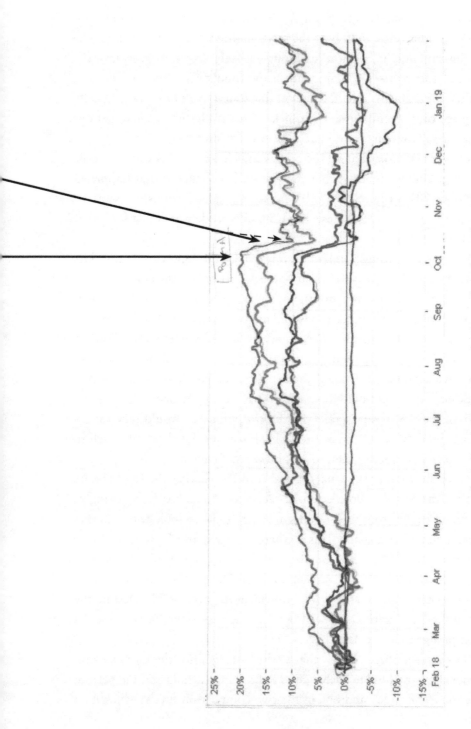

Chart B: one-year chart (built on data from the LSE)

When he or she gets to point A, the novice investor might say, 'Too right, I would invest – look how the stock has done since the spring!' The wiser investor might be more cautious – wisely so, as if you move the paper on, you will see a major fall in the fund's value. Note, however, that this fall looks like a cliff edge on this long-term graph, but actually took place over several days. The quick-witted trader had time to get out during the fall and buy back in at a lower price later.

You will also note that all the other funds fell too. This was not some disaster specific to the fund, but the big market shakeout that happened in October 2018. ('Fundamentals' investors argued furiously about the cause of this fall. Interest rates? The US/China trade war? I just looked at the chart.)

However, supposing you had been watching the fund closely, loved its performance and decided to buy at point A, just before the crash?

Firstly, if you followed my method, you would be investing slowly, building a position over time. You would not be fully invested at this time, so the loss would not be painful. If you had invested slowly but a little earlier, you would still be sitting on profits when the market turned. You could still have shown a gain if, for example, you had started building your holding in late spring and had got out half-way through the big October fall.

Given the run of sharp falls that follow point A, I would take this as a strong signal from the market to sell. This is not the chart on which to make a decision exactly when to sell, however. That's not its job.

You might look at the Chart A and wonder whether the fund lost its way after the October correction. It recovered a bit, but how strongly? It's difficult to tell from this long-term chart. Time to look at the market through a magnifying glass. This is where Charts B and C come in.

One of these (Chart B) covers a year, the other (Chart C) covers three months. How does the investment look on these? The one-year chart covers the correction. It shows the investment in good health. Despite the fall, the fund still performed well over the year. It looks like it took the market plunge in its stride.

However, the three-month chart, which starts after the October fall, does not show the fund in such a good light. Its value falls over the period, unlike the FTSE index and one of the two comparison funds, which gain in value.

Chart D, which covers the last four weeks of trading, shows the daily movements of the market. I call it my Buying Chart, as this is where I decide the exact timing of my investment decisions. It's not so much a magnifying glass as a microscope.

It shows that the fund is now clearly doing badly – all the other comparisons are doing better than it. I sometimes think of funds as a group of horses galloping across a beach. As an investor, you want to be riding the leading one, and if that starts to drop behind, you want to change horses. I would be very wary of holding this fund at this point and would be looking to change horses and seek opportunities elsewhere.

However, if I did wish to continue to invest in the fund, when would I buy? This is the chart to find out.

I've already spoken against the dangers of 'trying to catch a falling knife'. Wait till the market has reached a bottom and then buy. Of course, you can't know when this has happened, so rules of thumb have to be used. The classic one from Dow Theory is to buy after two consecutive upticks (an uptick, remember, is a day on which the price ends up higher than it started). On this graph, this happens on January 18th (a Friday) and the 21st. So you buy at the start of trading on the 22nd.

By the 28th, this doesn't look too clever, but from that time on, the price begins to rise, if only slowly. Should you want to add to your holding, Dow Theory would insist you wait until the morning of February 6th, as there are not two consecutive upticks until February 4th and 5th. (There are single, one-day upticks before that, but they are followed by downticks the next day – not enough to get the Dow Theory investor back into the market.) Impatient traders might shout out that this misses some of the rise – but over time, the Dow approach, together with my strategy of building a holding slowly, makes sure you fulfil my rules one and two. Protect your assets!

The Dow approach also takes away much of the stress of investing. Do I have difficulty making my mind up about a trade? No, because the chart makes my mind up for me.

You still have to exercise plenty of judgement in picking the right funds to trade in. As I've said, this choice should be the result of close study of the fund's performance over different timescales and relative to other well-performing funds.

Red = Global Growth Fund
Turquoise = Global Equity Growth Fund
Blue = UK FTSI 100
Light Magenta = (Low volatility) Money Market Fund
Dark Magenta = UK Small Caps

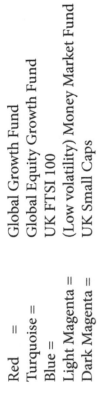

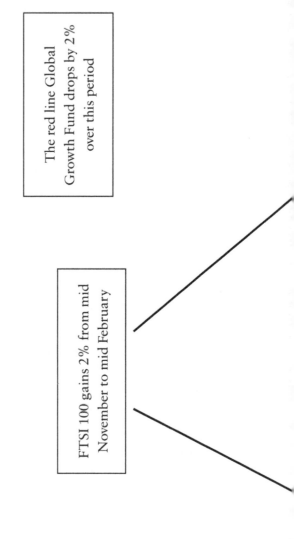

FTSI 100 gains 2% from mid November to mid February

The red line Global Growth Fund drops by 2% over this period

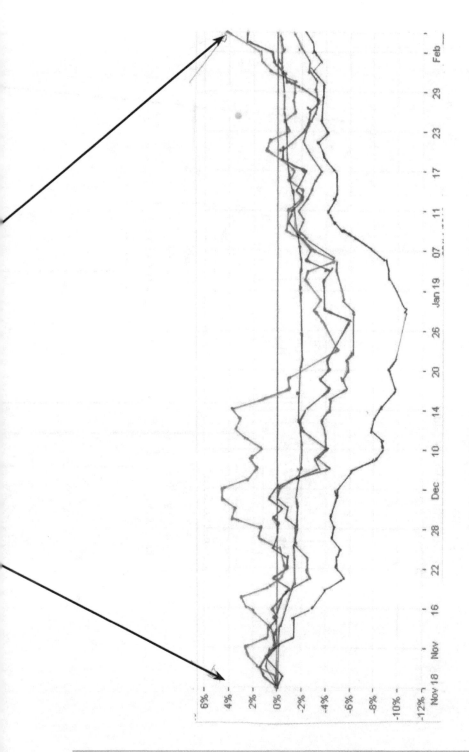

Chart C: three-month chart (built on data from the LSE)

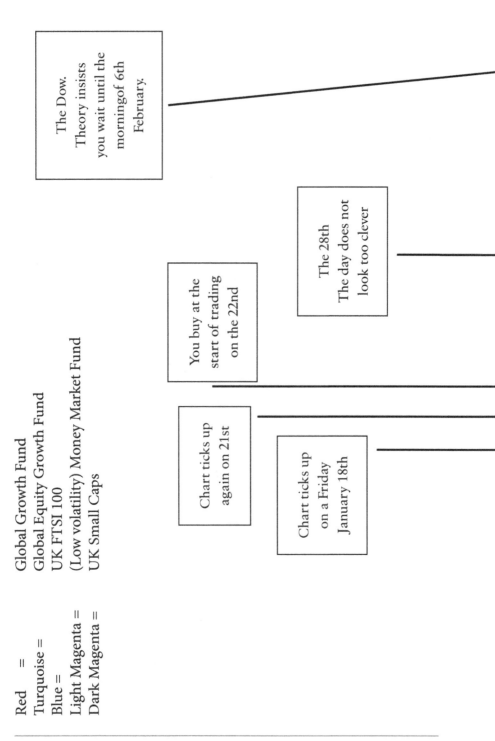

The Dow. Theory insists you wait until the morningof 6th February.

The 28th The day does not look too clever

You buy at the start of trading on the 22nd

Chart ticks up again on 21st

Chart ticks up on a Friday January 18th

Red = Global Growth Fund
Turquoise = Global Equity Growth Fund
Blue = UK FTSI 100
Light Magenta = (Low volatility) Money Market Fund
Dark Magenta = UK Small Caps

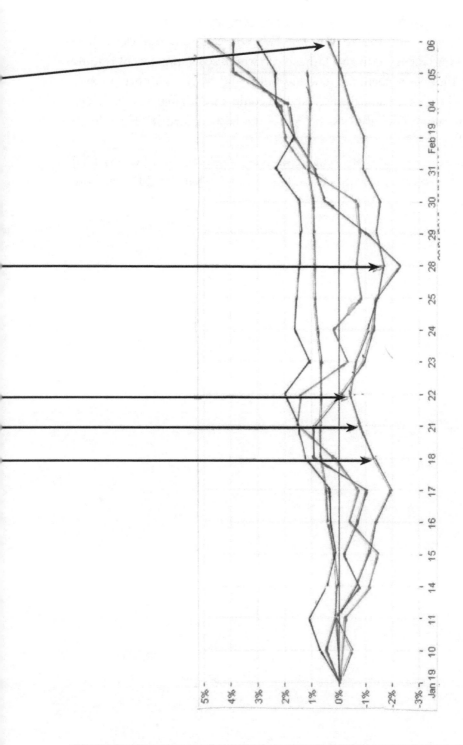

Chart D: four-week chart (built on data from the LSE)

Should you wish to sell your holding (or part of it) over this period, Dow Theory tells you to wait for two consecutive downticks. These happen on January 14th and 15th, so you would sell at the start of trading on the 16th. Since then, the fund has fallen and risen – but once you had sold, as long as the stock was clear, you could have 'changed horses'. The light turquoise Global Growth fund is the best performer on the long-term chart.

I must point out that I haven't set these charts up to prove any kind of point, just taken recent ones and tried to see what I could learn from them.

CHAPTER TWENTY-ONE
I DID IT MY WAY

Recently, a colleague of Caroline's offered us all the free use of a three-bedroom luxury apartment situated within a gated complex overlooking a golf course in Marbella. Caroline booked the flights and we were off – Pat, myself, Caroline and her son Harrison. It was truly 5-star accommodation: super-sized rooms, with fantastic views, its own pool, a large private outdoor verandah, quiet and peaceful – just what someone like me wanted.

We took things easy. In the afternoons, we would make a beeline for the sea front and the huge marble play area where you can hire all sorts of things on hourly terms: bikes, electric scooters, skate boards… Harrison liked hiring a bike, and would race against me in my buggy around this huge marble arena. He would always want to win and usually did: I devised a handicap system where he would give me a start. We had great fun. In the evenings, we would either go to a favourite restaurant, or Caroline and Pat would make something delicious back at the apartment.

The day before we were due to fly back, my life almost ended. I started an internal bleed and was coughing up blood big time: remember I am on permanent warfarin. Caroline and Pat acted promptly and ambulanced me into a private hospital. I really thought my time had come to depart this world, but I wasn't going to go easily; my determination kicked in. I had become used to this situation, so I remained calm. All the doctors in the hospital were first class; the first night I was in they thought I might not make it, so they put me in intensive care. I made it through the night, and they put me back into a ward the following day. I was still in a very fragile condition; I had three pints of blood and a pint of iron; I was very disorientated. At the end of the week, I was released. Wow, I had ducked another bullet – one's bound to hit me sooner or later. Caroline booked the flights home for the next day Sunday; we knew getting home would be very difficult for me so we planned for me to stay in my buggy and go extremely gently until I got into bed at home. Well, needless to say, I made it.

Seeing my grandson charging around on his bike, then coming face to face with my own possible end – it puts it all in perspective.

When I look back on my life now, I think of a quote from Geoff Capes, a British Olympic competitor, and once the World's Strongest Man: "When you have had nothing you value everything." I started out as a boy who thought that everyone in the world was better than me and that I was a nothing. Remember that earlier in this book I said my best friend was my Raleigh bike, then my Lambretta was my best friend. Now I have an electric bike, but to me now it's just a bike. My best friend now is Pat, the best person in the world. I have changed to a person with unrelenting self-belief; I hope this story has shown how. This could be seen by some as arrogance. I think there is a fine line between the two, but I would hate it for people to think I am arrogant, for I detest arrogant people.

At my birth I was not dealt Kings and Queens as many were. I got a poor hand, but luck was with me. I was dealt one Ace, for which I can thank my parents. Written across the face of the Ace, in large bold letters, is one word, DETERMINATION. It can be a very difficult card to play, as one has to keep using it all the time. Although I didn't know it at the start of this story, it would bring me success – success by my standards, a modest target by some people's.

I have had luck, too. I have always said that you make your own luck, and I still largely believe that. But I have also come to realise that there is also genuine random luck. For example, it was genuine luck the night I met Pat. I thought at the time that I could never trust anyone again for the rest of my life, but here was someone I could trust my life with. It was genuine luck that Mr Youhana gave me my first heart operation, for he was no quitter. He had determination. There have been other moments, mentioned in this story.

Have I acquired wisdom? Yes, a lot; I suspect more than most lads who were bottom of the class at school. I can give good guidance to the younger generation – but often they don't listen. I understand that in a way. When I was young, I didn't listen to the advice of people I didn't know and who thus hadn't earned my respect. Maybe I should have listened sometimes. The tears can come later.

There was a time when I would not turn the other cheek. I was never vindictive, but I would not give in. Now I am far more tolerant of others, even when they are very aggressive to the point of been physically intimidating. I will answer with a gentle smile, which can take them by shock, after which all of a sudden, almost like magic, they are often understanding and on my side. And if they are not, I don't let it get to me.

The other day, for example, Pat and I were looking for a blue badge holder's space in a parking zone. Pat stopped the car and got out to go and look; she found one about 80 meters away. I drove the car towards it, when suddenly another car came from the opposite direction, forced Pat to stand aside and took the space. I was furious. Pat said, 'Forget it; let's find somewhere else to park.' I hobbled over with my walking stick to the car window and knocked on it. Rather than get angry, I calmly explained the situation to the driver, a woman with a young child. However, she was not interested. Then I let it go. Years ago, I would never have been so tolerant – but I suddenly realised there was no point.

A boy who was messed around by his own family, I now find my own family a source of deep happiness. Harrison is my only grandchild. If it hadn't been for my surgeon Mr Youhana, I would never have seen or known about him, He is the life and soul of my life in this 'twilight zone' of mine, and Pat's pride and joy too.

I wanted him to have the best possible start in life (unlike myself). Pat and I discussed it with Caroline and we agreed to help her out and send Harrison to a private school. I had one in mind: Saint Michael's School, Llanelli, about ten miles away from home. It had an outstanding academic record.

The three of us took Harrison for the school to see him and for us to see them. We liked what we saw: all the staff were very caring, dedicated and professional. I was particularly interested in the ethos of the school. I said to the headmistress of the lower school that I wanted the school to get the best out of him that he could give, but also for him to be a considerate person towards others, in a nutshell a well-rounded confident person who would comfortable speaking to beggars and kings and treat them all the same.

He was too young to start there, however, so he began at the local state school – an eye opener for Caroline as she had been privately educated. (Incidentally, the difference between the schools is not just about money. Most of the buildings at St Michaels were ramshackle; I look all around me and see brand new schools everywhere, yet the standard of Welsh education is almost the worst in Europe!)

Caroline kept Harrison at the state school for a term and a half before starting him at Saint Mike's, as it's affectionately known. The education there lasts right up to A level. It is a school with small numbers, around 250 pupils who are all friends and mix with each other. Some are boarders, but Harrison is lucky; he's a day pupil; we wouldn't want it any other way. Unfortunately, Harrison is suspected of being dyslexic, just like myself and his Uncle Richard. In the 1940s, dyslexia meant you were a dunce, asked far too many questions which disrupted the class, and were ignored. Richard was lucky: his school recognised it and taught him how to handle it. Harrison is lucky, too: Caroline and the school help him to manage it. He is always first up with his hand to ask or answer pertinent questions. Mrs Rees-Davies, whose arm he has been under since starting at Saint Mikes, has seen it all before and says that once he cracks his problem he will be away in a shot.

What do I want from life in my closing years? I want to be happy and content, by having my family around me. I want my needs taken care of. I want to watch Harrison develop, as far as life permits me. We all love him to bits, spoil him to bits. I teach him manly things, and sometimes you have to be cruel to be kind, which understandably he doesn't like. I try to make it up later with a bit of fun, like playing hockey with my two walking sticks in my hallway with the doors at each end as the goals. We bully off in the middle. I am the ref, to stop him cheating, but he normally wins anyway with his superior mobility. O, such fun! I have ensured that when I am no longer here, Pat is well catered for – my lover and best friend.

I have some regrets, but I can look back and be proud to say, just like the Frank Sinatra song, that I did it my way.

Some Extras

1)   People I Admire from this Great Country of Ours

I shall list them in alphabetical order.

Anthony Wedgwood Benn. He gave up his inherited peerage to stand up
for what he thought was right, despite anyone else's thoughts, or what
the colours of their political party were. He settled down in Bristol,
becoming an MP. He was a great orator, who could convince anyone
of anything, and one of the few truly honest politicians. His son
Hilary is now following in his footsteps.

Aneurin Bevan. Born 15th November 1897, the son of a coal miner, he
did poorly at school, so much so that his headmaster made him repeat
a year. He left school at 13 and went to work in the local colliery.
He became active in politics, and in 1928 was elected Labour MP for
Ebbw Vale. As Minster of Health he introduced the National Health
Act 1946, free health service for all. This has become the cornerstone
for all nations to aspire to. To me he is the greatest Welshman ever.

Winston Churchill. Born 30th November 1874, of mixed English
and American parentage, into an aristocratic family, and a direct
descendant of the Duke of Marlborough, Winston Churchill began
school at the age of seven. He hated it. He did poorly academically

and misbehaved, and only just passed the entrance exam to study at the elite Harrow School. He was a better student there, especially in history, though staff complained he was unpunctual and careless.

His family lined him up for a career in the army, but he failed on his first attempt to get into the Royal Military Academy, Sandhurst. He got in at the second attempt, however.

He became a Conservative MP, for Oldham, in 1900, and later achieved high office. But in the mid-1930s, he became a lone, backbench voice in Parliament warning against the rise of Hitler.

On 10th May 1940, hours before the German invasion of France, he became prime minister. His speeches were an inspiration to the whole nation, as we stood alone against the might of the German Empire. "Let us therefore brace ourselves to do our duties and so bear ourselves, that if the British Empire and its Commonwealth last for a thousand years, men will still say, this was their finest hour."

Dow and Jones. I could not resist putting these on my list, even though they are not from Britain. They may not have military or political power, but every great country needs wealth to sustain it: he who pays the piper calls the tune. Charles Dow was born on November 6th 1851, was poorly educated, and lived with his family in the hills of Connecticut. His father died when Charles was six. Edward Davis Jones was born 7th October 1856, of Welsh descent, was co-founder of the Wall Street Journal. Both Dow and Jones were honest, in a world full of hucksters trying to manipulate markets, and Dow's thinking on how markets work is still incredibly insightful.

Nigel Farage. Born 3rd April 1964 at Downe, Kent, he was educated at Dulwich College, a private school in South London, from 1975 to 1982. On leaving school he decided not to go to university, but to work in the City trading commodities at the London Metal Exchange. He was active in politics from his school days, with the Conservative Party, but left it in 1992 in protest at John Major's signing of the Maastricht Treaty on European Union. Next year, he became a founding member of UKIP. In 1999, he was elected to the European Parliament, where he continues. He is considered one of the two best speakers in the chamber. On May 20 2014, Farage led UKIP to win the European Parliamentary Election in the UK, the first time in over 100 years that a political party other than Labour or the Conservatives has won an election.

Nigel Farage has fought almost single-handedly in the cauldron of the EU debating chamber in Brussels, standing his ground with dignity and fighting fiercely like the British bulldog that he is. He is not perfect: he can be brash and abrupt, which can make it difficult to win over people's support. Nevertheless he's a fighter, and won't give up until Britain has full sovereignty back. This was given away in 1973 without consulting the British people. One day, this man will stand shoulder to shoulder with Churchill, Nelson and Wellington, then we will have rainbows over the white cliffs of Dover. Just you wait and see!

Teresa May. Born 1st October 1956 in Eastbourne, Sussex. Her father Hubert Brasier was a Church of England clergyman and her mother a supporter of the Conservative Party. At the age of 13 she won a place at a state grammar school, then went on to the University of Oxford, where she read Geography. In 1977 she went to work for the Bank of England. In 1980, Teresa married Phillip May.

In the 1997 general election she was selected as the Conservative candidate for Maidenhead, and was duly elected. While in opposition she served in a number of shadow cabinet positions. After the 2010 election, she was appointed Home Secretary. In June 2016, she announced her candidateship for the leader of the Conservative Party, won that and as a result became prime minister. Addressing the world's media outside Downing Street, she gave a passionate and moving speech. What struck a chord with me was when she said, "If you are white working class boy you're less likely than anyone else in Britain to go to university." That brought tears to my eyes. I thought 'That's me in the 1940s', and that one line inspired me to write this book.

Admiral Nelson. Nelson was born on the 29th September 1758 into a moderately prosperous home. He joined the navy through the influence of an uncle. He then rose quickly through the ranks, and obtained his own command in 1778. Like Wellington, he developed a reputation of leading from the front and was a great tactician. During the period of the Napoleonic Wars, he was wounded several times, losing the sight of one eye in one encounter and one arm in another.

In 1805 he took over the Cadiz blockade from Rear Admiral

Collingwood on the 21st October. The Franco-Spanish fleet came out of port, and they faced each other for the Battle of Trafalgar. The plan was for the British to charge directly at the opposing fleet, which was lined up in a crescent shape directly in front of them. The ships were in two single lines, one led by Nelson with the flagship Victory, the other led by Collingwood. Collingwood, whose ship was faster than Nelson's due to being plated with a copper bottom, pierced the enemy line first, targeting their flagship. Soon after, HMS Victory joined the battle, with the rest of the fleet bravely on its heels. However, as Victory joined the battle, a sniper from a French boat targeted Nelson, and he was mortally wounded.

At this point Collingwood took charge. Other leaders or forces might have buckled: at this vital moment the British were vulnerable. But it never showed, due to the high calibre of Collingwood, his men and their officers. As great as Nelson is, Collingwood should be given more credit for his participation in the battle, too.

The Duke of Wellington. Born in Dublin during May 1769 into an aristocratic Anglo Irish family – his father was Arthur Wellesley, 1st Earl of Mornington. His early schooling was in Dublin; later on he enrolled at Eton College, studying from 1781 to 1784. Like Churchill at Harrow, he hated it. In 1785, his lack of scholastic success coupled with a shortage of funds caused him to leave.

Together with his mother they went to live in Brussels. He obtained a commission in the army in 1787, through family connections. These also enabled him to be elected as a Member of Parliament for Trim in the Irish House of Commons in 1793. In the same year, he became a major – by buying the rank – and later in the same year he purchased the rank of Lieutenant Colonel. Hardly an impressive start in life.

However, thereafter he was promoted on merit, rising to the rank of field marshal. He fought all over the British Empire, getting a reputation as a strategist who cared for his men and led by example from the front. In many battles he would beat what appeared to be overwhelming odds. Wellington is most famous for beating Napoleon Bonaparte at Waterloo. Typical of Wellington's thoroughness, he had visited the site of the battle one year previously, and carefully chose a defensive position which would prove decisive in the eventual victory.

2) Rudyard Kipling's 'If' (full text)

If you can keep your head when all about you
Are losing theirs and blaming it on you;
If you can trust yourself when all men doubt you,
But make allowance for their doubting too:
If you can wait and not be tired of waiting,
Or been lied about don't deal in lies,
Or been hated don't give way to hating,
And yet don't look to good, nor talk too wise;

If you can dream – and not make dreams your master;
If you can think – and not make thoughts your aim,
If you can meet with triumph and Disaster
And treat those two imposters just the same:
If you bear to hear the truth you've spoken
Twisted by naves to make a trap for fools,
Or watch the things you gave your life to, broken,
And stop and build 'em up with worn-out tools;

If you can make one heap of all your winnings
And risk it all on one turn of pitch and toss,
And lose and start again at your beginnings,
And never breathe a word about your loss:
If you can force your heart and nerve and sinew
To serve your turn long after they are gone,
And so hold on when there is nothing in you
Except the will which says to them: "Hold on!"

If you can talk with crowds and keep your virtue,
Or walk with Kings – nor lose the common touch,
If neither foes nor loving friends can hurt you,
If all men count with you but none too much:
If you can fill the unforgiving minute
With sixty seconds' worth of distance run,
Yours is the earth and everything that's in it,
And which is more – you'll be a man my son!

Fantastic, something to aspire to. If I can pick one line out it is:

Trust yourself when all men doubt you

3) Books to read (on investment)

Trading for a Living by Dr Alexander Elder
Come into My Trading Room by Dr Alexander Elder
Study Guide for Come into My Trading Room by Dr Alexander Elder
The Warren Buffett Way by Robert G. Hagstrom, Jr.
Charting Made Easy by John J. Murphy
Technical Analysis of the Financial Markets by John J. Murphy
Japanese Candlestick Charting Techniques by Steve Nison

ACKNOWLEDGEMENTS

I would like to thank various people for their support. Without them, The Golden Money Tree would never have been penned.

Pat, Caroline, Richard and all my family, for their mental support to me when the going was tough. Julie Barnes, for proof reading the medical side; Edwin Jones for proof reading the investment side as a 'man-in-the-street' investor; and last but no means least, my book guru, Chris West, who with immense patience and encouragement, guided me, a hugely dyslexic person with a forceful personality, and helped me write this book. He polished it and polished it to both our satisfactions. His own knowledge of financial markets was very helpful, too.

Thank you all.